ALSO BY MARTHA C. NUSSBAUM

Aristotle's De Motu Animalium

The Fragility of Goodness:
Luck and Ethics in Greek Tragedy and Philosophy

Love's Knowledge: Essays on Philosophy and Literature

The Therapy of Desire: Theory and Practice in Hellenistic Ethics

Poetic Justice: The Literary Imagination and Public Life

Cultivating Humanity:
A Classical Defense of Reform in Liberal Education

Sex and Social Justice

Women and Human Development: The Capabilities Approach

Upheavals of Thought: The Intelligence of Emotions

Hiding from Humanity: Disgust, Shame, and the Law

Frontiers of Justice: Disability, Nationality, Species Membership

The Clash Within:
Democracy, Religious Violence, and India's Future

Liberty of Conscience:
In Defense of America's Tradition of Religious Equality

From Disgust to Humanity:
Sexual Orientation and Constitutional Law

Not for Profit: Why Democracy Needs the Humanities

The New Religious Intolerance:
Overcoming the Politics of Fear in an Anxious Age

Creating Capabilities: The Human Development Approach

Political Emotions: Why Love Matters for Justice

Anger and Forgiveness: Resentment, Generosity, Justice

Aging Thoughtfully: Conversations about Retirement,
Romance, Wrinkles, and Regret (with Saul Levmore)

THE MONARCHY *OF* FEAR

A PHILOSOPHER LOOKS AT OUR POLITICAL CRISIS

MARTHA C. NUSSBAUM

SIMON & SCHUSTER

NEW YORK LONDON TORONTO SYDNEY NEW DELHI

Simon & Schuster
1230 Avenue of the Americas
New York, NY 10020

First Simon & Schuster hardcover edition July 2018

Interior design by Ruth Lee-Mui

Manufactured in the United States of America

1 3 5 7 9 10 8 6 4 2

Library of Congress Control Number: 2017049444

ISBN 978-1-5011-7249-6
ISBN 978-1-5011-7250-2 (ebook)

To Saul Levmore

Contents

Preface

Election night 2016 was bright daylight for me—in Kyoto, where I had just arrived for an award ceremony, after a joyful sendoff from my colleagues at home. I was feeling pretty anxious about the bitterly divided electorate, and yet reasonably confident that appeals to fear and anger would be repudiated—although there would be a lot of difficult work ahead to bring Americans together. My Japanese hosts came in and out of my hotel room, explaining the schedule of the various ceremonial events. In the background of these conversations, but in the foreground of my mind, the election news kept coming in, producing, first, increasing alarm and then, finally, both grief and a deeper fear, for the country and its people and institutions. I was aware that my fear was not balanced or fair-minded, so I was part of the problem that I worried about.

I was in Kyoto to accept an award established by a Japanese scientist, businessman, and philanthropist—also a Zen Buddhist priest—who wanted to recognize "those who have contributed significantly to the scientific, cultural, and spiritual betterment of mankind." While I loved the fact that Dr. Kazuo Inamori recognized philosophy as one of the disciplines capable of making a major contribution, I felt the award as more a challenge than an accolade, and was already wondering how, at this fraught moment in US history, I might actually live up to my laurels!

By the time the election result was clear, I had to go out to have my first official meeting with the other two laureates (both scientists) at the offices of the Inamori Foundation, so I dressed up in a cheerful suit, fixed my hair, and tried to express happiness and gratitude. The first official dinner was a chore. Social conversation with strangers, filtered through an interpreter, offered no distracting charms. I wanted to hug my friends, but they were far away. Email is great, but not like a hug for comfort and consolation.

That night the combination of political anxiety and jet lag made sleep somewhat intermittent, so I began thinking—deciding, around midnight, that my previous work on emotions hadn't gone deep enough. As I examined my own fear, it gradually dawned on me that fear was the issue, a nebulous and multiform fear suffusing US society. I got some ideas, tentative but promising, about how fear is connected to, and renders toxic, other problematic emotions such as anger, disgust, and envy. I rarely work in the middle of the night. I sleep soundly, and my best ideas usually come to me gradually, sitting at my computer. But jet lag and a national crisis have a way of changing habit, and in this case, I had a joyful sense of discovery. I felt that some insight might possibly be the fruit of this upheaval—and who knows?—it might be insight that would give others some good ideas, too, if I could do the work well. I went back to sleep with a calming sense of hope.

The following day—after a cleansing morning workout—I plunged into formal ceremony. I donned my evening dress and smiled as best I could for the official portrait photo. The onstage ceremony was aesthetically beautiful and hence distracting, and listening to the biographies of my fellow laureates and their short speeches about their work was genuinely fascinating, since they were in fields (self-driving cars and basic cancer research) about which I know little, and I was filled with admiration for their achievements. Giving my own short speech, I was able to express some of the things I really care about and to thank people who had helped me throughout my career. At least as important, I could also express love of my family and close friends. (All this had to be written in advance for the sake of the translator, so no *ad hoc* modification was possible, but being able to express love was still extremely consoling.)

Kyoto prize banquets end punctually and extremely early, so by 8:30 I was back in my room, and I sat down at my desk and wrote. By that time the ideas I had had during the night had taken form, and as I wrote, they became more and more developed and more and more convincing (at least to me!). By the end of two evenings of work, I had a long blog piece that a journalist friend of mine in Australia posted, and that blog piece simultaneously took a different shape as a book proposal.

But who am I, you might ask, and how did I come to take such a keen interest in the emotions of political unity and division? I am, of course, an academic, living a highly privileged life in the midst of wonderful colleagues and students, and with all the support I could wish for my work. Even at this time of grave threat for the humanities and the arts, my own university still strongly supports the humanities. As a philosopher without a law degree, I have the great delight of serving partly in a law school, where I can learn every day about the political and legal issues of this nation, meanwhile offering courses about justice and political ideas. So, it's a fine vantage point, but it might seem too detached to participate in the anxieties of most Americans.

I was a privileged child, too, but in a far more complicated way. My family, living on Philadelphia's elite Main Line, was upper middle-class and fairly affluent. I had love, excellent nutrition and health care, a first-rate education at an excellent private school for women, which in those days supplied incentives to excellence, free of gendered peer pressure, that a public-school education would have offered to girls only more unevenly. (My mother used to tell me, "Don't talk so much, or the boys won't like you," apt advice for the times, but I didn't have to worry about following it at school!) I've always loved reading, writing, and constructing arguments. Furthermore, my father loved my aspirations and supported them. A working-class man from Macon, Georgia, he had worked his way up to a partnership in a leading Philadelphia law firm by dint of ability and hard work, and he thought and said that this American Dream was available to all. That credo planted seeds of doubt. He repeatedly said that African Americans failed to succeed in America because they just didn't work hard enough; and yet, observing his own visceral racism, as he made household help use a separate bathroom, and even threatened to disinherit me if I appeared in public in a large group (a theater troupe) one member of which was African American, I saw that his credo did not make sense of the situation of African

Americans, held down and insulted by stigma and Jim Crow separation. And my father's disgust with minorities extended to many who plainly had (despite social obstacles) achieved success through hard work: to middle-class African Americans and middle-class Jews in particular.

He understood that women could excel. He delighted in my success, and encouraged independence and even defiance. And yet I observed an issue there, too: for he married a woman who was working as an interior designer, and it was immediately understood that she would stop working, something that left my mother unhappy and lonely for much of her life. His attitudes were so mixed. When I was sixteen, he offered me the choice between a debutante party and a homestay abroad on the Experiment in International Living, and was thoroughly pleased that I chose the latter—but he would never have married a woman who didn't choose the former. He did think that wearing daring fashionable clothes was (for both women and men) thoroughly compatible with intellectual aspiration and success, and the fun we had on shopping expeditions was doubled by the subversive plan that I would show up at his lecture on "Powers of Appointment" at the Practising Law Institute wearing a bright pink mini-suit. And yet, where did he really think all of this was heading? To what sort of family life, in particular? He encouraged me to date exactly those upwardly mobile preppy men who—like him—would never have wanted a working wife.

Meanwhile, that trip abroad fed further my skepticism about my father's credo. I was sent to live with a family of factory workers in Swansea, South Wales, and I understood how poverty, bad nutrition, bad sanitation (no indoor plumbing), and bad health conditions (coal mining in particular, which had ruined the health of quite a few family members) robbed people not only of flourishing lives but also of desire and effort. My teenage pals in that family did not want to go to school or to excel by hard work. Like the working-class British families relentlessly studied in Michael Apted's "7 Up" and its sequels, they envisaged for themselves no rosier future than the lives of their parents, and their greatest pleasure was to go drinking and to visit the legal gambling casinos nearby. I remember lying in bed reading an elite British novel—in that house with an outhouse in the garden—and thinking about why Eirwen Jones, my own age, hadn't the slightest interest in reading and writing, or even in learning Welsh. The obstacles imposed by poverty often lie deep in the human spirit, and many deprived people can't follow my father's path. (By his own account, he was well nourished, given a lot of love, inspiration, and good health care, and somehow got a first-rate education. He didn't notice how being white gave him huge advantages. Born in 1901, he also lived in a world of greater upward mobility than is now the case, even for poor white people.) So, I saw myself in a new perspective, as not just a very smart kid but as the product of social forces that are unequally distributed. It wasn't surprising that much later I deepened this understanding through work in an international development institute and by a deep partnership with development groups working for women's education and legal rights in India.

Like most of the people I knew in Bryn Mawr, I was at that time a Republican, and I admired the libertarian ideas of Barry Goldwater. I still believe Goldwater was an honorable man and totally committed to the eradication of racial segregation—he had in fact boldly integrated his family business. I think he really believed that people should choose to be just and should respect and help one another, only without government coercion. But when I began working for his campaign while still in high school, I discovered that most of my fellow Goldwaterites were not high-minded but deeply racist, supporting libertarianism as a screen for segregationist views. The ugliness of white supremacist politics repelled me, convincing me that Goldwater was naïve and that only the force of law would finally break the grip of Jim Crow. I also understood by then (after that homestay in Swansea) that real equality requires equal access to nutrition and health care. I began to embrace the political ideals of the New Deal, while my father protested to my school that my history teachers had "brainwashed" me—not the only time he underestimated the independence he had proudly nourished.

I've mentioned the theater, and early in my life the arts, especially theater and music, became my window onto a more inclusive world. First of all, it was a world that encouraged the expression of powerful emotions, unlike the WASP culture of Bryn Mawr. All my teachers encouraged my mind, but the drama teacher encouraged my whole personality. I decided that I wanted to be a professional actress. I did summer stock for two seasons, left Wellesley College after three semesters to take a professional job in a repertory company, and pursued acting at what is now the Tisch School of the Arts at NYU (New York University)—until I understood that I was not a very good actress, that the life was too unstable, and that my real passion was thinking and writing about the plays. But I still act and sing as an amateur (I'm better, having had real-life experience), and it brings me joy. I also urge my colleagues to act (in plays connected to our law-literature conferences). I've found that sharing emotions with one's colleagues humanizes the law school and enriches intellectual friendship.

It was in the theater that I first encountered people who were openly gay. Indeed, I had a big crush on one such actor at the age of seventeen, and observed his life with the keen sympathy of disappointed infatuation, seeing how he had a life partner who visited him and with whom he had exchanged high school rings, but that they were openly together only in the world of the theater, not in the larger society. This seemed to me utterly absurd and irrational. He was certainly much nicer than most of the boys I knew, more understanding and respectful. I guess by that time I understood the ugly self-interest behind racism and sexism, but discrimination on the basis of sexual orientation, previously hidden from me as were the phenomena, was another appalling American vice I then added to my list.

After deciding not to become a professional actress, I returned to the academic side of NYU, where I thrived. And soon after that I met my future husband, got engaged, and converted to Judaism. I was and am attracted to the primacy of social justice in Judaism. And I have always loved the Jewish culture I joined, finding it more emotionally expressive and more openly argumentative than WASP culture. As one of my Jewish colleagues (highly successful) said of his own history in "white-shoe" law firms, WASP lawyers would never criticize you, just fire you suddenly after five years, whereas Jewish lawyers would yell and jump up and down, but in the end, treat you pretty fairly. Though no longer married, I've kept my Jewish name and my Jewish religion, and am more involved in the life of my congregation than I was back then. (With the middle initial *C*, I honor my birth name, Craven.) So that meant that I joined one of the groups my father despised, and he did not come to my wedding, although my mother helped organize it. (By that time my parents were divorced.)

I've had a charmed life in some respects, then, but early on I gradually learned to see it as privileged and to ponder the exclusions of others. One form of discrimination I did not avoid was discrimination against women, which played a major role in my early career (though I had a lot of encouragement, too), and which probably explained my not getting tenure at Harvard—although in a narrow decision, and with two departments split, any number of things could be brought forward to explain the result. And, like most working women of my generation, I've experienced the problems of reconstructing family life around expectations that were new and not yet fully explored. Even when both parties have the best intentions, male expectations of an earlier era are hard to live down in the heart, particularly when there are children. And sometimes two people who love one another just cannot manage to live together. But I certainly don't regret plunging in. My daughter, now a lawyer working for the rights of wild animals at Friends of Animals in Denver, is among the great joys of my life. (Her lovely and supportive husband, who was imprisoned in East Germany for three years, at the age of eighteen, for putting up one political poster criticizing Communism, has shown me the perspective of an immigrant, one who loves the United States, with its freedoms and its tradition of welcome and inclusion.)

Academics can be too detached from human realities to do good work about the texture of human life. That's a risk inherent in academic freedom and tenure, wonderful institutions that did not protect philosophers of most earlier eras. My own commitments and efforts have always led me to want to restore to philosophy the wide set of concerns that it had in the days of the Greeks and Romans: concerns with the emotions and the struggle for flourishing lives in troubled times; with love and friendship; with the human life span (including aging, so well studied by Cicero); with the hope for a just world. I've had a lot of partners in this search for a human philosophy (and several superb mentors, including Stanley Cavell, Hilary Putnam, and Bernard Williams). But I'm hoping that my own history, both in its unearned privileges and in its awareness of inequalities, has helped my search as well.

Maybe if I had been able to hug my friends, that night in November 2016, I would not have embarked on this book project, or not right then. But once I started down this path, my friends have been crucial sources of support, understanding, skeptical challenges, and useful further suggestions. Deference is poison to intellectual work, and I am so lucky that my colleagues and friends are far from deferential. But there is one above others whose skeptical challenges, provocative insights, cynical scoffing at all emotions, and unwavering support and friendship make me enjoy my life and work more and (I hope) do the work better. So I dedicate this book to Saul Levmore.

THE
MONARCHY
OF
FEAR

1

INTRODUCTION

There's a lot of fear around in the US today, and this fear is often mingled with anger, blame, and envy. Fear all too often blocks rational deliberation, poisons hope, and impedes constructive cooperation for a better future.

What is today's fear about? Many Americans feel themselves powerless, out of control of their own lives. They fear for their own future and that of their loved ones. They fear that the American Dream—that hope that your children will flourish and do even better than you have done—has died, and everything has slipped away from them. These feelings have their basis in real problems: among others, income stagnation in the lower middle class, alarming declines in the health and longevity of members of this group, especially men, and the escalating costs of higher education at the very time that a college degree is increasingly required for employment. But real problems are difficult to solve, and their solution takes long, hard study and cooperative work toward an uncertain future. It can consequently seem all too attractive to convert that sense of panic and impotence into blame and the "othering" of outsider groups such as immigrants, racial minorities, and women. "They" have taken our jobs. Or: wealthy elites have stolen our country.

The problems that globalization and automation create for working-class Americans are real, deep, and seemingly intractable. Rather than face those difficulties and uncertainties, people who sense their living standard declining can instead grasp after villains, and a fantasy takes shape: if "we" can somehow keep "them" out (build a wall) or keep them in "their place" (in subservient positions), "we" can regain our pride and, for men, their masculinity. Fear leads, then, to aggressive "othering" strategies rather than to useful analysis.

At the same time, fear also runs rampant among people on the "left," who seek greater social and economic equality and the vigorous protection of hard-won rights for women and minorities. Many people who were dismayed by the election are reacting as if the end of the world is at hand. A majority of my students, many acquaintances, many colleagues, feel and say, often with anguish, that our democracy is on the verge of collapse, that the new administration is unprecedented in its willingness to cater to racism, misogyny, and homophobia. They fear, especially, for the possible collapse of democratic freedoms—of speech, travel, association, press. My younger students, especially, think that the America they know and love is about to disappear. Rather than analyze matters soberly and listen to the other side, trying to sort things through, they often demonize an entire half of the American electorate, portraying them as monsters, enemies of everything good. As in the book of Revelation, these are the last days, when a righteous remnant must contend against Satanic forces.

We all need, first, to take a deep breath and recall our history. When I was a little girl, African Americans were being lynched in the South. Communists were losing their jobs. Women were just barely beginning to enter prestigious universities and the work force, and sexual harassment was a ubiquitous offense that had no laws to deter it. Jews could not win partnerships in major law firms. Gays and lesbians, criminals under law, were almost always in the closet. People with disabilities had no rights to public space and public education. Transgender was a category that had, as yet, no name. America was far from beautiful.

These facts tell us two things my students need to know. First, the America for which they are nostalgic never existed, not fully; it was a work in progress, a set of dynamic aspirations put in motion by tough work, cooperation, hope, and solidarity over a long period of time. A just and inclusive America never was and is not yet a fully achieved reality. Second, this present moment may look like backsliding from our march toward human equality, but it is not the apocalypse, and it is actually a time when hope and work can accomplish a great deal of good. On both left and right, panic doesn't just exaggerate our dangers, it also makes our moment much more dangerous than it would otherwise be, more likely to lead to genuine disasters.

It's like a bad marriage, in which fear, suspicion, and blame displace careful thought about what the real problems are and how to resolve them. Instead, those emotions, taking over, become their own problem and prevent constructive work, hope, listening, and cooperation.

When people are afraid of one another and of an unknown future, fear easily gives rise to scapegoating, to fantasies of payback, and to poisonous envy of the fortunate (whether those victorious in the election or those dominant socially and economically). We all remember FDR's statement that "we have nothing to fear but fear itself." We recently heard departing President Obama say, "Democracy can buckle when we give in to fear." Roosevelt was wrong if we take his words literally: although we had reason to fear fear, we certainly had many other things to fear in his time, such as Nazism, hunger, and social conflict. Fear of those evils was rational, and to that extent we should not fear our fear, though we should always examine it. But Obama's more precise and modest statement is surely right: giving way to fear, which means drifting with its currents, refusing skeptical examination, is surely dangerous. We need to think hard about fear and where fear is leading us. After taking a deep breath we all need to understand ourselves as well as we can, using that moment of detachment to figure out where fear and related emotions come from and where they are leading us.

But you might not be convinced, so far, that fear is really a deep problem for democratic self-government. Let me, then, imagine a little dialogue between me and a defender of fear, whom I'll call DF.

DF: But surely, we don't want to extinguish fear. Without fear we'd all be dead. Fear is useful, propelling us into life-saving action.

MN: Of course, you are right there. But fear has a strong tendency to get ahead of us, propelling us into selfish, heedless, and antisocial actions. I'll try to show you that this tendency comes from the evolutionary history and psychological structure of that emotion. More than other emotions, fear needs careful scrutiny and containment if it is not to turn poisonous.

DF: I'll need to be convinced. But I also want to know right now why you say that fear is particularly dangerous to democratic self-government. Surely democracies are often well advised to consult fear in thinking of how to structure laws and institutions. Isn't our defense establishment a sensible response to the legitimate fear of foreign domination? And what about our Constitution? Weren't the Framers guided by fear when they wrote the Bill of Rights? After all, they wrote down all the things that the British had violated or taken from them: their fear that similar things would happen in the new nation gave good, not bad, guidance to democracy.

MN: It would be stupid to deny that fear often gives good guidance. Fear, after all, is part of our evolutionary equipment for survival. But your examples involve fear filtered by careful and extended public deliberation. You've omitted hasty and ill-justified military campaigns. You've omitted cases where rights were unequally bestowed, or privileges hastily curtailed, as a result of popular fear. We have a habit of scapegoating unpopular people in times of national stress, and abridging their rights in ways that later seem completely misguided. Eugene Debs was thrown in jail for peaceful speeches opposing US involvement in World War I. Loyal and peaceful Japanese Americans were interned in camps. These are cases where fear not only did not lead in the direction of constitutional rights, but actually abridged rights that were established, and the same climate of fear prevented even our courts from seeing this at the time. Fear has a way of running ahead of careful thought. It's that stampede to hasty action, prompted by insecurity, that I view with great skepticism. Fear of that sort undermines fraternity, poisons cooperation, and makes us do things we're deeply ashamed of later.

DF: Once again, I await your arguments! You've persuaded me that there's a problem, but I don't yet see how large it is, or what its solution might be. But here's another thing you must try to clarify for me. You use the title "the monarchy of fear." And you keep saying that fear poses a special problem for democratic self-government. What I don't get is the particular connection you seem to be tracing between fear and a threat to *democracy*. To the extent that fear is a problem in society, doesn't it threaten all forms of government equally?

MN: Actually, no. In an absolute monarchy, the monarch, of course, can't be excessively fearful, although he or she had better not be excessively rash either. But monarchs feed on fear from below. Fear of the monarch's punishment ensures compliance. And fear of outside threats ensures voluntary servitude: fearful people want protection and care. They turn to a strong absolute ruler in search of care. In a democracy, by contrast, we must look one another in the eye as equals, and this means that a horizontal trust must connect citizens. Trust is not just reliance. Slaves can rely on a master's brutal behavior, but of course they do not trust the master. Trust means being willing to be exposed, to allow your own future to lie in the hands of your fellow citizens. Absolute monarchs don't need or want trust.

Think about a marriage. In an old-style marriage, in which the male head of household was like a monarch, there was no need for trust. Spouse and children just had to obey. But the marriages to which people typically aspire these days are more balanced, requiring genuine vulnerability, reciprocity, and trust on both sides. And trust is undermined by fear. To the extent that I see you as a threat to my life and my goals, I will protect myself against you, and I will be inclined to strategize, even dissemble, rather than trusting.

So too in politics. That refusal of trust is happening all over the country now. My students don't trust anyone who voted for Trump, and they view such people as like a hostile force, "deplorables" at best, fascists at worst. Many Trump supporters return the compliment, seeing students and universities as subversive enemies of "real people."

And here's another side to the connection. When people feel fearful and powerless, they grasp after control. They can't stand to wait to see how things play out, they need to make other people do what they want them to do. So, when they are not seeking a benign monarch to protect them, they are all too likely to behave monarchically themselves. Later I'll trace this tendency to the way that babies try to make slaves of their caregivers: realizing their own powerlessness, what can they do but scream? In this way too, fear erodes the sort of equal give and take, the reciprocity, that is needed if democracies are to survive. And it leads to retributive anger, which divides when what is most needed is a constructive and cooperative approach to an uncertain future.

DF: You mentioned anger. This makes me ask another question: why this emphasis on fear? Aren't there many emotions that threaten democracy? What about anger, in fact? Shouldn't we worry about that emotion even more than about fear, given its aggressive tendencies? Isn't it a sense of being treated unfairly that makes many Americans strike out at others? People also often think of envy as a major threat to democracy, fomenting class conflict. Finally, there's been a lot written about the role of disgust in racism and other forms of stigma and discrimination.

MN: You are entirely right there, and the chapters of this book will indeed address these different emotions and their interconnections. But having worked for many years on each emotion more or less in isolation from others, I've come to realize that my previous strategy obscured some very important causal relations among the emotions. In particular I've come to realize, and I'll try to convince you, that fear is primary, both genetically and causally, and that it is because of infection by fear that the three other emotions you named turn toxic and threaten democracy. Yes, sure, people strike back out of a sense of unfairness. But what is that exactly? Where does it come from? Why do people feel this way, and under what conditions does blame become politically toxic? These are the sorts of questions that we need to ask about each emotion, and I believe that they all lead back to fear and life-insecurity.

DF: But why all this fuss about emotions? Surely the big problems in American society are structural, and we need structural solutions, which can be implemented through law whether people feel good about them or not. We don't have to wait for people to become better, or more self-aware, in order to fix the things that need fixing, and focusing on emotions can even distract us from the structural work that needs to be done.

MN: I totally agree that structures and laws are crucial. I have views about those issues, which will emerge. But laws can't be enacted, or sustained, without the hearts and minds of people. In a monarchy, that is not the case, and all the monarch needs is enough fear to produce obedience. In a democracy we need much more: love of the good, hope for the future, a determination to combat the corrosive forces of hatred, disgust, and rage—all fed, I claim, by fear.

DF is not satisfied, and should not be, since only assertions have been offered so far, not argument or analysis. Still, DF should by now have a general sense of where my argument is heading. The problems of our time—economic, social, security-related—are complicated, resisting easy solutions. We hardly know where work is going or what it is likely to look like over the next few decades. The rising costs of health care also pose incredibly difficult challenges for any party or leader. Higher education, increasingly crucial for stable employment, is getting more and more out of reach for many of our citizens. The confusing politics of the Middle East and the Far East need to be understood by all Americans but resist easy analysis. Thinking is hard, fear and blame are easy.

DF might, though, have a more fundamental question: Why should we turn to a philosopher at all, at this time of crisis? What is philosophy all about, and how can it help us?

Philosophy means many things in many different historical traditions, but for me philosophy is not about authoritative pronouncements. It is not about one person claiming to be deeper than others or making allegedly wise assertions. It is about leading the "examined life," with humility about how little we really understand, with a commitment to arguments that are rigorous, reciprocal, and sincere, and with a willingness to listen to others as equal participants and to respond to what they offer. Philosophy in this Socratic conception does not compel, or threaten, or mock. It doesn't make bare assertions, but, instead, sets up a structure of thought in which a conclusion follows from premises the listener is free to dispute.

Socrates questioned lots of people in the Athenian democracy. He found that all had the capacity for understanding and self-understanding. (Plato dramatizes this by showing Socrates questioning an illiterate and oppressed slave boy, and, suitably prompted, the boy comes up with a sophisticated geometrical proof.) Philosophical questioning assumes that basic capacity, but it also shows that most of us neglect its cultivation: people (including, as Socrates found, military leaders, cultural authorities, and politicians) don't really sort out what they think, and they rush to action on the basis of half-baked, frequently inconsistent, ideas. In that way, philosophy invites dialogue and respects the listener. Unlike the overconfident citizens that Socrates questioned (Euthyphro, Critias, Meletus), the philosophical speaker is humble and exposed: his or her position is transparent and thus vulnerable to criticism. (His or her, since Socrates said he'd like to question women, if only in the afterlife, and Plato actually taught women in his school!)

Socrates was right to say that his method was closely linked to the goals of democratic self-government, in which each person's thought matters, and to insist that it made a very valuable contribution to life in a democracy, improving the quality of public deliberation. He said he was like a gadfly on the back of the democracy, which he compared to a "noble but sluggish horse": the sting of philosophical questioning was supposed to wake democracy up so that it could conduct its business better.

This is not a book of public policy, or of economic analysis, crucial though both of these disciplines are to solving our problems. It is more general, and more introspective. It aims at a better understanding of some of the forces that move us, and to that extent it offers general directions for action. But understanding is its primary goal. Understanding is always practical, since without it action is bound to be unfocused and ad hoc.

Philosophers talk about many topics that have relevance to democracy. My own work, like a lot of philosophical work in the past few decades, has discussed political institutions and laws, making general arguments about what justice is and what basic rights or entitlements all citizens have. I'll allude to some of those ideas about human empowerment and "human capabilities" in my chapters on preventing envy and constructing hope, suggesting that they may give us help as we move forward, but this won't be the primary focus of this book.

The other half of my career has focused on the nature of the emotions and their role in our search for the good life. Following a long tradition stretching (in Western philosophy) from Plato on through modern thinkers such as Adam Smith and John Rawls, I have argued (drawing on psychology and psychoanalytic thought as well as philosophy) that emotions have an important role to play in a decent political society. Emotions can destabilize a community and fragment it, or they can produce better cooperation and more energetic striving toward justice. Emotions are not hardwired from birth, but are shaped in countless ways by social contexts and social norms. That is good news, since it means that we have considerable room to shape the emotions of our own political culture. It is also bad news—for the lazy and uninquisitive: it means that we need to inquire into the nature of fear, hatred, anger, disgust, hope, and

love, thinking about how we might shape them so that they will support good democratic aspirations, rather than blocking or eroding them. We can't avoid accountability by saying of our own hatred or excessive fear, "Sorry, that's just how people are." No, there is nothing inevitable or "natural" about racial hatred, fear of immigrants, a passion to subordinate women, or disgust at the bodies of people with disabilities. We did this, all of us, and we can, and must undo it.

In short, we need to know ourselves and take responsibility for ourselves. It is incumbent on a decent society to give attention to how, for example, group hatred can be minimized by social efforts and institutional design. Even such a straightforward policy choice as the choice to mainstream children with disabilities in "normal" classrooms has evident consequences for patterns of fear and aggression. We need to study the issue—in this case and in many others—and then, on the basis of what we understand, to choose policies that produce hope, love, and cooperation, avoiding those that feed hatred and disgust. Sometimes we can only produce better behavior, while hatred continues to simmer beneath the surface. Sometimes, however, we can actually alter how people see one another and feel about one another—as mainstreaming kids with disabilities surely does. (It helps to start young.)

Philosophy doesn't all by itself dictate very many concrete policy choices, because these must be contextual, the fruit of a partnership between philosophy, history, political science, economics, law, and sociology. But it gives us a sense of who we are, what problems lie in our path, and where we should be heading. And as I said, its methods, involving equal

participation, respect, and reciprocity, also model some important aspects of where we should be going. It is a part of the study of our political moment, not the whole, but it can help us all to lead the "examined life."

Philosophy, as I've said, is a gentle discipline. It approaches people with respect for their full humanity, and is in that sense a form of love. It may frequently state unequivocally, "This is wrong. This is not the way to live." But it does so without banishing people from the room, condemning wrong beliefs and bad actions, but treating people, always, with attention and respect. I believe that it is not too bold to link the philosophical approach to America's problems with the methodology of nonviolent political change, as exemplified in the life and work of Martin Luther King Jr. Some approaches to political change are violent, angry, and contemptuous of the opponent. King (who will be an important figure in this book) insisted on an attitude to others that he called Love, even when what he was doing was to make an extremely vigorous protest against unjust conditions. Still, he said, we must approach opponents not with anger but with love. He always immediately stressed that it was not romantic love, and it did not even require us to like the people. The Love he demanded was a combination of respect for humanity with good will and hope: we treat people as people who will listen and think, and who ultimately may join with us in building something beautiful. Philosophy, as I shall practice it here, shares that project and that hope.

My argument begins, not surprisingly, with fear, showing how it is both chronologically and causally primary, getting its

teeth into us very early and then coloring the rest of our lives to a greater or lesser degree. This analysis already shows some strategies for containing fear and rendering it less poisonous, although it also concludes that we can't get rid of its dangers entirely.

I then consider three emotions that operate to some extent independently of fear in our private and public lives, but that become especially toxic when infused by fear: anger, disgust, and envy. I first analyze each of them and then show their bad effects in democratic political life.

I then devote a separate chapter to negative political emotions directed at women, which have been extremely prominent in our recent political discourse. I analyze the relationship between sexism (which I define as a set of views asserting that women are inferior to men) and misogyny (which I define as an enforcement strategy, a type of virulent hatred and hatred-behavior aimed at keeping women "in their place"). I argue that misogyny, which usually rests on sexist convictions but need not, is typically a toxic brew of punitive anger, bodily disgust (not incompatible with sexual desire), and envy at women's increasing competitive success.

Finally, I turn—or return, since each chapter has included constructive suggestions for containing or overcoming the damaging aspects of each emotion—to hope, love, and work. I am guardedly optimistic about our future, and a philosophical analysis of hope suggests strategies for nourishing hope, faith, and love of humanity, just when it seems especially difficult to believe that these good emotions might possibly guide us.

Throughout, although I do use some recent political

examples to underscore my points, my aim is to invite reflection, introspection, and critical argument. To that end, I more often use historical examples—especially from ancient Greece and Rome, where I have a long background of scholarship. As I've found in teaching, we often think better, and relate to one another better, when we take a step back from the daily, where our immediate fears and wishes are likely to be at stake.

2

FEAR. EARLY AND POWERFUL

You are lying on your back in the dark. Wet. Cold. Hunger and thirst throb and throb. They are you, and you are nothing but pain. You try to scream, and you somehow make a sound come out—but nothing happens. You try, or start to try, to move, to go somewhere, anywhere, out of this agony. But your limbs won't move. You can't make them do anything but wave uselessly in the air. You see, you hear, you feel. But you can't move or act. You are completely, simply, helpless.

This is the stuff of nightmare. Most of us have nightmares of helplessness, in which we try to run away from some terrible danger, but our legs won't move, or we try to scream but no sound comes out, or nobody hears it. In those nightmares we feel a terrible fear of the bad people or monsters who are pursuing us, but an even greater fear, and maybe also hatred, of our own powerlessness.

But this horror story is also the unremarkable daily life of every human baby. Calves, colts, baby elephants, puppies, giraffes, dolphins—all other animals learn to move very quickly, more or less right after birth. If they can't stand upright, nurse, and, very soon, walk or swim alongside the mother, using their own bodies to get the food that they need, they are severely defective, and they will almost certainly die. Helplessness means the end. Human beings alone are helpless for a very long time, and human beings alone survive that helpless condition. As the first-century BCE Roman poet Lucretius, one of my favorite guiding spirits in thinking about emotions, puts it, the baby

> like a sailor cast forth from the fierce waves, lies naked on the ground, unable to speak, in need of every sort of help to stay alive, when first nature casts it forth with birth contractions from its mother's womb into the shores of light. And it fills the whole place with mournful weeping, as is fitting for one to whom such trouble remains in life.(5.222–7)[1]

[1]Titus Lucretius Carus lived from around 99 to 55 BCE, thus during the beginning of the long decline of the Roman Republic into tyranny. A disciple of the Greek philosopher Epicurus (341–270 BCE), he created a six-book epic poem in dactylic hexameters to disseminate Epicurus's teachings about fear, aggression, and the structure of the universe. Since he had access to more of Epicurus's writing than we do, it is difficult to say how much he innovated, but certainly all of the brilliant poetic imagery and at least some of the philosophy (especially portions reconciling Epicureanism with Roman values) is his own. There are many good translations. In this book I make my own, rather flat-footed and literal, but my favorite to

Other animals, he drily remarks, have no need of rattles or baby talk; they don't need different clothing for different seasons. They don't need to arm themselves, they don't need high city walls. After all, the earth and nature herself provide everything that any other animal needs.

We come into a world that we are not ready to cope with. (And in a crucial sense we never really are.) Terribly soft and vulnerable, we lie there helpless, waiting for others to provide what we need—food, comfort, and reassurance. After the soothing undulations of life in the womb, its automatic nourishment and unproblematic excretion, there is suddenly a violent separateness, the slap of the cold air, and a painful solitary powerlessness. The discrepancy between the very slow physical development of the human infant and its rapid cognitive development is in many respects a nightmare story.[2] You see what you need, but you can't move to get it. You feel pain, but you cannot remove it. Later nightmares no doubt recall this early torment. Neurological research on fear concludes that the scars of early fright stimuli endure, resisting change.[3]

And you really are aware of what is happening to you.[4] By

---

capture the spirit of the poetry is that of Rolfe Humphries (Bloomington: Indiana University Press, 2008).

[2]A brilliant re-creation, based in detail on what we now know from research, is psychologist Daniel Stern's *Diary of a Baby* (New York: Basic Books, 1990); a more prosaic version is in his *The Interpersonal World of the Infant* (New York: Basic Books, 1985).

[3]See discussion of LeDoux below.

[4]My views therefore reject Freud's simple hedonism, which does not attribute to infants much in the way of awareness of objects; here, as in other work, I follow the "object-relations" school of thinkers such as W. R. D.

the age of one month an infant can tell the difference between its own parents and other people, although it is only much later that it can really see a person as a whole person or understand that the flashing images of movement in and out of its field of vision are stable substances. Indeed, it takes months even to grasp the distinction between parts of the infant's own body (feet, hands) and physical objects outside its body. Infants constantly experiment with sameness and externality, grabbing their own toes, putting into their mouths first parts of themselves (thumbs, fingers) and parts of non-self (blanket ends, pacifiers). Still, all of that learning unfolds—and mere yelling gradually becomes semi-articulate syllables—long before an infant can walk, or even crawl, on its own.

We usually survive this condition. We do not survive it without being formed, and deformed, by it. Fear, genetically first among the emotions, persists beneath all and infects them all, nibbling around the edges of love and reciprocity.

There are good times, too. As Lucretius understands, the world of pain is also a world of delight. "Into the shores of light" is where we have come, into a world of amazing beauty and excitement. Light entrances, and virtually an infant's first voluntary movement is to follow light with its eyes. But incipient joy and love are soon overwhelmed by the pain of need.

There are also times of a quieter comfort. You suck at the

Fairbairn and especially Donald Winnicott, who is now the dominant force in US psychoanalytic training. Melanie Klein is close to this school but a unique figure defying categorization. Detailed discussions of the views of all three are in my *Upheavals of Thought: The Intelligence of Emotions* (New York: Cambridge University Press, 2001), ch. 5.

breast or bottle. You are held on a warm body that smells a little sweet, a little salty. You are enclosed by soothing arms. But you didn't make that happen. Somehow it just happened to you, and you have as yet no sense of how you could make it happen when you need it. Even when you begin to discover that screaming is regularly followed (after an interval) by feeding and comfort, it's still not as if you can comfort or feed yourself. The only way you can get what you need is to make some other part of the world get it for you.

Politics begins where we begin. Most political philosophers have been males, and even if they had children they did not typically spend time with them or observe them closely. Lucretius's poetic imagination already led him to places where his life probably did not. But philosophy made big steps when one of democracy's great early theorists, Jean-Jacques Rousseau (1712–1778), a major intellectual architect of the revolutionary anti-monarchical politics of the eighteenth century, wrote about the education of children with a deep understanding of the psychology of infancy and its dangers for the democratic project.[5] Rousseau was the opposite of a loving parent: indeed he sent all his children (four or five, all illegitimate) to a foundling hospital on birth, and did not even record their dates of birth. Somehow, though, through his various experiments in teaching other people's young children, through conversations with

[5]Rousseau's views are not mine; his *On the Social Contract* prescribes a coercive homogeneity of thought and speech under the rubric of the "civil religion," not making room for the liberties of speech, press, and association that were so dear to his US counterparts and to British thinkers such as John Locke and, later, John Stuart Mill.

women, through memories of his own childhood, through his close reading of Lucretius and other Roman philosophers, and through his own poetic imagination, he understood how early need creates problems for the type of political order he sought.

Human life, Rousseau understood, begins not in democracy but in monarchy. The baby, on whom caregivers ardently dote, has no way of surviving except by making slaves of others. Babies are so weak that they must either rule or die. Incapable of shared work or reciprocity, they can get things only by commands and threats, and by exploiting the worshipful love given them by others.[6] (In letters, Rousseau made it clear that this was why he abandoned his children: he just didn't have time to be at a baby's beck and call.)

What emotions begin to take root in the infant's unfolding life? In the womb it's hard to speak of emotions, although toward the end there are eventually sensations—because emotions require some awareness, however confused, of external objects and some thoughts, however rudimentary and unformed, about those objects. Emotions, then, fit the post-birth world in which we are separated from the sources of good, longing for their presence, dimly aware that they are out there somewhere, uncontrolled by us. To the infant trapped in this nightmare

[6]Rousseau, *Emile: or On Education*, trans. Allan Bloom (New York: Basic Books, 1979), Book I, pp. 62–67, esp. p. 66: "Thus, from their weakness, which is in the first place the source of the feeling of their dependence, is subsequently born the idea of empire and domination." Rousseau believes that one can begin resisting this fearful dependence very early, by encouraging free movement and self-sufficient care of self. I don't follow the details of his views, but develop his initial insight in my own way, influenced by psychologists like Stern and especially by the views of Winnicott.

scenario, one overwhelming emotion, and a formative influence on daily life, is fear. Adults are amused by the baby's futile kicking and undisturbed by its crying, since they know they are going to feed, clothe, protect, and care for it. They respond to its evident need for comfort by holding it close, by speaking baby talk (known even in ancient Rome!), by making rocking motions, simulating the safety of the womb. But adults themselves don't fear, because they don't think anything bad is going on—unless there are other danger signals such as fever or inability to tolerate milk. The infant's world, however, knows nothing of trust, regularity, or security. Its limited experience and short time horizons mean that only the present torment is fully real while it lasts, and moments of joyful reassurance, fleeting and unstable, all too quickly lead back into insufficiency and terror. Even the joy itself is soon tainted by anxiety, since to the infant it seems fleeting, all too likely to slip away.

DEFINING FEAR

Philosophers are fond of definitions, and so are psychologists. Within each field there is disagreement about fear, but a common ground of consensus has emerged, in the light of recent interdisciplinary research on both human and animal emotions. This consensus includes the idea that almost all emotions (in both humans and other animals) involve some sort of information processing about the animal's well-being. Even non-linguistic animals have thoughts, in some form, of what's good and bad for them, and these thoughts are incorporated into their emotions. Thus, emotions are not like mindless jolts of energy: they focus outward on the world and appraise objects and events in the world. Typically, they register our animal vulnerability, our dependence on and attachment to things outside ourselves that we do not fully control. (This is why the ancient Greek and Roman Stoics were in favor of eliminating almost all emotions, apart from some, like wonder at the universe, or a serene joy at one's own integrity, that did not seem to them to involve an unwise dependence on "goods of fortune.")[7]

Fear is not only the earliest emotion in human life, it is also the most broadly shared within the animal kingdom. To have compassion you need a pretty sophisticated set of thoughts: that someone else is suffering, that this suffering is bad, that it would be good for it to be relieved. Some animals have this emotion (apes, elephants), but it requires relatively complex thinking. To have full-blown anger, rather than just irritation or primitive rage, you have to be capable of causal thinking: someone did something to me, and it was wrong. But to have fear, all you need is an awareness of danger looming. Aristotle defined fear as pain at the seeming presence of some impending bad thing, combined with a feeling that you are powerless to ward it off.[8] That's pretty good. The thoughts involved don't require language, they only require perception, and some sense, however vague, of one's own good or ill. Something bad is looming, and I am stuck.

[7]I build a case for this overall view, drawing on both philosophy and psychology, in *Upheavals of Thought: The Intelligence of Emotions* (New York: Cambridge University Press, 2001). Some parts of my picture are controversial, but not the general ideas expressed here.
[8]Aristotle, *Rhetoric* II.5, 1382a21–5.

What about feelings? Fear is certainly accompanied by some powerful subjective feelings; often people mention a "trembling" or a "shaking." Should we put that into the definition, saying that if that isn't there, the emotion can't really be fear? There are three reasons why we should not. First, different people experience fear differently, depending on their history and character. Do we really want to say that a courageous soldier must be trembling in his boots if he retains a normal human fear of death? Aristotle said that even the most courageous do fear death, and they'd be crazy not to.[9] We don't want soldiers who hold life cheap. But in the case of the disciplined soldier, the awareness of danger isn't usually felt as a trembling.

We can go even further: in many cases people have fear without even being aware of it. Every day, most of us are motivated in quite a lot of what we do by the fear of death. We don't walk in front of cars (unless we hold our smartphones dearer than life!). We try to guard our health, we go to the doctor, etc. The fear of death is often very useful, but it is usually non-conscious, just like the belief in gravity, or the belief in the solidity of physical objects—non-conscious, but everywhere relied on.

We don't need a psychoanalytic doctrine of repression to tell us that fear often lurks beneath the surface of the mind. But I think that we can, and should, go further: it is of the essence of peaceful daily life that we push that fear to the back of our minds. Lucretius, probably the first theorist of unconscious fear, remarks that this effort sometimes becomes a burden.

[9]Aristotle, *Nicomachean Ethics* III.9, 1117b7–16.

So instead of a trembling, we may have a feeling of a "large mountain sitting on our chest." Or we have frenetic avoidance behavior, restless activity that seems aimed at nothing but self-distraction. Think of air travel. Some people have a conscious fear of flying. Many more of us, however, push that fear to the back of our minds but still feel an inner weight or tension, and a more than usual need to distract ourselves with email, or food, or aimless conversation. We may be simply more irritable than usual, or less able to concentrate.

Finally, scientists tend, these days, to agree with Aristotle, who was a great biologist and who theorized a lot about the emotions of animals: all animals, not just humans, feel fear of something bad out there that seems likely to harm them.[10] It's generally believed that fear evolved because of its role in keeping animals alive. But if we are to talk about the way fear feels to a rat, what should we say it feels like? We can be sure that animals have rich subjective experience, but it would be very rash to pretend to know what they feel.

Fear does involve feelings, then, but it's hard to define fear in terms of any particular type of feeling. We are on safer ground when we stick to the sort of awareness of objects as good or bad that seems an unavoidably central part of fear, and necessary to explain animal behavior. So, let's by all means say that the subjective side of fear is important, and let's call poets and novelists to our aid in describing its many types and instances. But let's focus, for now, on the awareness of objects that holds all the cases together.

[10]Aristotle, *Historia Animalium*, many references throughout.

What about the brain? Here we need to learn from recent research. In his important book *The Emotional Brain: The Mysterious Underpinnings of Emotional Life*,[11] neuroscientist Joseph LeDoux has given a masterful account of how the emotion of fear has a particularly close connection with the amygdala, an almond-shaped organ at the base of the brain. When creatures report fear, or their behavior is reasonably explained as fear, the amygdala is aroused. And LeDoux has also shown that certain specific triggers elicit fear-related responses in humans, no doubt through stored evolutionary mechanisms: the shape of the snake, for example, always gets the amygdala going.

The amygdala is an unusually primitive organ. All vertebrates have it, no matter what the level of the rest of their perceptual and cognitive apparatus, and have it in recognizably the same form. Clearly, the role of the amygdala helps explain why fear belongs to all animals. In experiencing fear, we draw on a common animal heritage, and not just a primate or even vertebrate heritage. Fear goes straight back to the reptilian brain.

LeDoux is careful not to say that fear is "in" the amygdala, or that knowing about the amygdala's role fully explains fear. First of all, he has not experimented on humans. Second, he is perfectly aware that in all animals, fear relies on the entire network and that the amygdala functions only in virtue of its role in a more complex system. If this is true in rats, it is all the more likely to be true for humans. Humans' information about danger comes from many sources, perceptual, linguistic, intellectual. Moreover, the human brain is reasonably plastic, and

[11]New York: Simon and Schuster, 1996.

there are likely to be many differences among individuals in the ways their brains process a single emotion.

We can't have a good account of fear by simply describing brain states, then. A good account will need to speak about creatures' subjective awareness of objects, and their vague or inchoate thoughts of situations or objects as bad for the self (which might itself be a vague inchoate concept in most animals and in human infants). This awareness is mediated, as time goes on, by learning. We learn the map of our world, and learn what is good and bad in it. This makes fear seem more human and less primitive. Still, it's worth emphasizing that fear is an emotion that a rat can have in not too different a form from a small human. Rats too have a mental map of good and bad, though without language or higher thought. And even if our first primal experiences of fear are followed, later, by complicated, learned forms of that emotion, LeDoux emphasizes that early fright conditioning has lasting effects on the organism; it proves very difficult to undo. We all know how fear swells up in times of danger, how it drives our dreams.

FEAR'S POLITICS

Fear is not just primitive, it is also asocial. When we feel compassion, we are turned outward: we think of what is happening to others and what is causing it. We don't ascribe compassion to an animal unless we think that it is part of some rich social network. Dogs, apes, and elephants probably do care compassionately about the fortunes of other creatures in their world. Scientists who work on these species conclude that they have complicated forms of social awareness, and the emotions that go with that. But you don't need society to have fear; you need only yourself and a threatening world. Fear, indeed, is intensely narcissistic. It drives out all thoughts of others, even if those thoughts have taken root in some form. An infant's fear is entirely focused on its own body. Even when, later on, we become capable of concern for others, fear often drives that concern away, returning us to infantile solipsism. Soldiers describe the experience of fear in combat as involving a vivid inward focus on their whole body, which becomes their whole world.[12] (This is why military training has to focus so obsessively on building team loyalty—because it has to counter a deep contrary tendency.)

Or think of our anxious interactions with the medical profession. When we get threatening medical news—or even when we go for a regular checkup and think we might possibly get some bad news—we are likely to be totally self-focused and on high alert. (The common experience of a rise in blood pressure at the doctor's office is one sign of the return of helplessness-anxiety.) Often, of course, we do fear for our children and other loved ones, and are on high alert for them. But that just means that the self has become bigger, and the intense painful awareness of danger to your larger self drives out thought of the wider world.

The great novelist Marcel Proust imagines a child (his

[12]One remarkable depiction is in Erich Maria Remarque, *All Quiet on the Western Front*, trans. Brian Murdoch (London: Random House, 1994; original German publication 1929), p. 37. Remarque served on the Western Front for several months at the age of eighteen, before being seriously wounded in combat; he spent the rest of the war in an army hospital.

narrator) who remains unusually prone to fear, especially at bedtime.[13] What project does terror suggest to young Marcel? That he should make his mother come to his room, stay, and leave as late as possible. (He notes that the comfort of her presence is already tainted by the awareness that she is soon to depart.) Marcel's fear makes him need to control others. He has no interest in what would make his mother happy. Dominated by fear, he just needs her to be at his command. This pattern marks all his subsequent relationships, particularly that with Albertine, his great love. He cannot stand Albertine's independence. It makes him too anxious. Lack of full control makes him crazy with fear and jealousy. The sad result, which he narrates with great self-knowledge, is that he feels secure with Albertine only when she is asleep. He never really loves her as she is, because as she is she is not his own.

Proust supports Rousseau's point: fear is the emotion of an absolute monarch, who cares about nothing and nobody else. (Rousseau thought the kings of France could not have compassion for the people they rule, since they could not imagine any type of common world, or reciprocity, with them.[14]) It didn't have to be that way. Other animals can act on their own almost as soon as they fear, and their fear, so far as we can tell, remains within bounds and doesn't impede concern and cooperation. Elephants, for example, are acting reciprocally with their herd group almost from birth. They run to adult females for comfort, but they also play games with other young elephants or

[13]Proust, *Remembrance of Things Past*, trans. C. K. Scott Moncrieff and Terence Kilmartin (New York: Vintage, 1982), vol. I.
[14]See *Emile*, book IV.

with adults, they gradually learn the emotion vocabulary that makes elephant life peculiarly communal and altruistic.

The human baby, powerless, has only one way of getting what it wants: using other people.

CONCERN, RECIPROCITY, PLAY

How do infants overcome the narcissism of fear? Our bleak narrative must now become more subtle, because we know that we are much more than that imperious baby, forcing others to do its bidding. And thinking about how we extricate ourselves from infantile narcissism might help us think about how to extricate ourselves from our very narcissistic and anxiety-driven political moment.

Times of comfort and delight give rise to love and gratitude. These emotions are both developmentally later and structurally more complicated than fear. Love that is more than narcissistic need requires the ability to think about the other person as a separate person, to imagine what that other person feels and wants, and to allow that person a separate, non-slave life. It involves, then, a move out of monarchy in the direction of democratic reciprocity.

This movement is uneven, lurching, and uncertain, but the ability to imagine another person's life aids it, as does a return of love prompted by the caretakers' evident love and good will. Probably gratitude and reciprocal love have an evolutionary basis. The bonding between parents and children that is necessary for species survival requires at least limited reciprocity. Parents need to feel that they get some return for all their investment—a reason why care for children with profound emotional disabilities (severe autism, for example) is so agonizingly difficult. In prehistory, such children would probably have been abandoned. Psychologists doing experimental work on infants (Yale's Paul Bloom in particular) believe that the ability to enter the world of the caretaker—to be a "mind reader"—arrives very early. That ability is clearly essential for normal human adulthood.[15] Robert Hare's study of psychopaths concludes that the absence of "mind reading" and of genuine reciprocal concern are hallmarks of these deeply maimed individuals, who are probably born, not made.[16]

Still, the rest of us all have tendencies that mimic psychopathy, in the form of our normal human narcissism. All too often we don't stop to think about what our words and actions mean for the inner lives of others. Maybe we can't even figure it out, if the others are very different from us. All too often, even when we do make an effort, it is for people in a narrow circle, our family, our group: for that "larger self" I spoke of—so our use of our own moral capacities remains fundamentally narcissistic. And all too often, even when we know full well what our words and actions mean for others—that they will inflict pain or humiliation, or impose a difficult burden—we just don't care. The narcissistic anxious world in which we began swells up again in time of need and fear, jeopardizing our halting steps toward moral adulthood and constructive citizenship.

[15]See Paul Bloom, *Descartes' Baby: How the Science of Child Development Explains What Makes Us Human* (New York: Basic Books, 2004).
[16]Robert D. Hare, *Without Conscience: The Disturbing World of the Psychopaths Among Us* (New York: Guilford Press, 1999).

Eighteenth-century philosopher Adam Smith, an early opponent of both colonial conquest and the slave trade, observed that it is difficult for people to sustain concern for people at a distance, when fear can so easily call the mind back to the self. His example is an earthquake in China. Hearing of the disaster, a humane person in Europe will be extremely upset and concerned—for a while. But if that same person hears that he (Smith typically imagines males) will lose his little finger the following day, he will completely forget the fate of millions of people: "the destruction of that immense multitude seems plainly an object less interesting to him than this paltry misfortune of his own."[17]

What can early interactions with children do to make our steps toward others a little less halting? Thinking about this will give us our first clues to productive social responses.

So long as the young child feels helpless, unable to be alone without fear, reciprocity and love will not flourish. Donald Winnicott, a great psychoanalyst who was also a pediatrician, observing thousands of healthy children, concluded that the dark story of terror and monarchical enslavement rarely prevails.[18] Life usually works out better than that, albeit uneasily and with much backsliding. Gradually, the infant develops the capacity to be alone. How does this happen? One key thing Winnicott

[17] Adam Smith, *The Theory of Moral Sentiments* (Indianapolis: Liberty Classics 1982), III.3.5, p. 136.

[18] Winnicott was a prolific writer, but especially important for this chapter are *The Maturational Processes and the Facilitating Environment* (Madison, CT: International Universities Press, 1965), and *Playing and Reality* (Abingdon: Routledge, 1971).

observed was the role of what he called "transitional objects," the blankets and stuffed animals that very young children use to comfort themselves when parents are absent. (He loved Charles Schulz's *Peanuts* and wondered whether Linus's blanket showed the influence of his ideas.) Cuddling a blanket or teddy bear calms fear, and so the child does not need to boss its parents around so much; the groundwork for what Winnicott called "mature interdependence" begins to be laid.

Eventually the child usually develops the ability to "play alone in the presence of its mother," amusing itself without needing to call for the parent all the time, even though he or she might be within sight or earshot. (Winnicott made it clear that "mother" was a role not a specific gendered person; he prided himself on his own maternal qualities, and often identified with female characters in books and movies.) Security and confidence begin to make healthy reciprocity possible.

At this point, a child begins to be able to relate to its parents as whole people, rather than as an extension of its own needs. The democratic self is ready to be born.

This stage, Winnicott thought, typically leads to a painful emotional crisis: for the child now understands that the very same person whom it loves and embraces is the person against whom it has directed its aggressive and angry wishes when its needs met with frustration. But here real moral life begins: for out of dismay at its own aggression, the child gradually develops a "capacity for concern": the parent must not be destroyed, and I must become the sort of person that does not destroy. Morality operates in tandem with love, since it is love that leads the child to feel the badness of its own aggression. Imaginative play, Winnicott thought, plays a key role in this development. Through stories, songs, and games, enacting stories happy and scary with stuffed animals, dolls, and other toys, children make a map of the world's possibilities and of the insides of other people. They start to become capable of generosity and altruism. Winnicott always emphasized the ethical and political role of the arts, which continue, for adults, the healthy role of play in the young child's life. "We are poor indeed," he said, "if we are only sane."[19]

Children cannot achieve emotional maturity on their own. They need stable and loving care, and care of a sort that reassures them that even their fear and aggression do not cancel the parent's love. Overcoming fear—to the extent that we ever can—is a relational matter. Love and holding supply the first phase of what Winnicott calls the "facilitating environment." The parent must receive the child's hate and not be terrified or depressed—and Winnicott emphasized that most parents do this well enough. He or she must "continue to be herself, to be empathic towards her infant, to be there to receive the spontaneous gesture, and to be pleased."

But if we thought of young childhood as a happy place full of games, toys, and teddy bears, we would be fooling ourselves. The horrible darkness of early fear is always beneath the surface, easily awakened into nightmare by any destabilizing new development: a childhood illness, the illness or death of a parent, the birth of a new sibling.

Gabrielle was two and a half when her parents brought her

[19]Winnicott repeated this phrase periodically, but one instance is in *The Family and Individual Development* (London and New York: Routledge, 1965), 61.

to Winnicott for treatment.[20] After the birth of a younger sister, the little girl was crippled with anxieties and nightmares. Their central theme was a terrible dark danger menacing her, somehow connected to the new baby and her parents' attention to her. She imagined a horrid dark train called a "babacar" carrying her to some unknown place. A "black mommy" loomed over her, trying to hurt her, but was also inside her and made her black. Worst of all was the "Sush baba," a nightmare version of the new infant. (Her baby sister's name was Susan.)

Gabrielle (known in the analysis by her nickname, "the Piggle") had loving, attentive, and playful parents. Her father even joined the analysis, and there is a lovely description of how, at Winnicott's urging, he mimed the birth of the new child by sliding down Winnicott's body onto the floor. She was obviously an unusually sensitive child; not all children are crippled by anxiety at such "normal" events. But it's important to remember that the fears that brought Gabrielle to Winnicott are in all children to some degree, even if they manifest themselves less severely, or are less noticed by sensitive and observant parents. Her story is unique; but it can also stand for all of us, since young childhood is a time of recurrent fear and insecurity.

The analysis continued at periodic intervals (dictated by the child's own requests) until Gabrielle was five. Winnicott's notes show that a key to the analysis was his utter respect for the child's inner world and his remarkable ability to enter

[20]D. W. Winnicott, *The Piggle: An Account of the Psychoanalytic Treatment of a Little Girl* (London: Penguin, 1977).

into it. Almost his first remark, in notes of the first session, is, "Already I had made friends with the teddy-bear who was sitting on the floor by the desk." Winnicott made both Gabrielle and her parents feel secure, establishing an atmosphere of "holding" in which fear could gradually be expressed and ultimately abate. The game in which her father pretended to be a baby is a typical example of Winnicott's creative insight: for if the father mimes the terrors of infancy, thus making himself vulnerable—and does so, I would add, in a comic way, producing laughter and delight—this helps the child manage her own fears. Similarly, the helpless fear and aggression that Gabrielle feels toward the new baby is made into a funny game, in which she hits Winnicott with a pretend rolling pin. The game gives her perspective, helping her to master her aggression.

At the end of the analysis, Gabrielle has to bid farewell to Winnicott himself, a potential trauma. As the two sit together, Winnicott remarks, "So the Winnicott you invented was all yours and he's now finished with, and no one else can ever have him." (In this way he reminds Gabrielle that they have a unique relationship. She was afraid that her baby sister would displace her in her parents' love, and now she is bound to be afraid that new patients will displace her in Winnicott's love. But that's not how love works—it is a unique bond, he says.) The two sit together, reading an animal book. Then he says, "I know when you are really shy, and that is when you want to tell me that you love me." "She was very positive in her gesture of assent."

In 2017, Deborah Luepnitz, an analyst in Philadelphia, corresponded with a fellow therapist, who then chose to reveal herself as "Gabrielle." Luepnitz then did a long interview with her, recently published.[21] Gabrielle had herself become a psychoanalytic therapist. She told Luepnitz that in her view it was highly significant that her mother's family were Czech Jews and refugees from the Holocaust. (Her father was an Irish protestant.) Gabrielle's own real name was Esther. The parents, it turns out, were themselves still so paralyzed by fear that they were unable to call her by her real name, which, as she puts it, "holds the family's Jewish history and trauma." She remembers relatively little of the analysis, but she does remember the game with the rolling pin, and how she felt guilty because she knew Winnicott had been sick and she had made him "play very hard." It is striking that this moment of awakening concern for the other is her sharpest memory.

THE FACILITATING ENVIRONMENT, PART I

Gabrielle's case reminds us that childhood is inherently a terrifying time. Concern, love, and reciprocity are staggering achievements, won against fierce opposition. Winnicott concluded that most parents, by far, do a good job. Children don't need perfection, and the demand for perfection often makes parents stressed out in a way that harms both parent and child. They only need holding that is "good enough." But Winnicott lived through two world wars and saw many children

[21]Deborah Anna Luepnitz, "The Name of the Piggle: Reconsidering Winnicott's Classic Case in Light of Some Conversations with the Adult 'Gabrielle,' " *International Journal of Psychoanalysis* 98 (2017), 343–70.

traumatized by separation, absence, and violence. (Maybe Gabrielle's mother had unwittingly transmitted to her child some of the terror of the Holocaust that she evidently felt: the "babacar" seems eerily like German transport trains.) He also knew well that parents can inflict deep emotional or even physical abuse on their children. He himself was harmed by a pathologically depressed mother and a cruel father who taunted him for his gender nonconformity.[22] He said that this "violation of the self's core" was more painful than "being eaten by cannibals." Its result was that he was sexually impotent until middle age—when he met his second wife Claire, a social worker, gender nonconforming in her own way, and also funny, kind, and joyful. So Winnicott knew that the baseline conditions for surmounting fear without damage are not always met.

Winnicott invented a concept for what children need, if concern for others is to grow and flourish. He called these conditions the "facilitating environment." In a first phase, he applied this concept to the family: it must have a core of basic loving stability (as his own did not). It must be free from sadism and child abuse (as his was not). But the minute we think about families in wartime, we also see that the facilitating environment has economic and social preconditions as well: there must be basic freedom from violence and chaos, from fears of ethnic persecution and terror; there must be enough to eat and basic health care. Working with children evacuated from war zones, he understood the psychic costs of external chaos. So

[22]For all the material in this section, see F. Robert Rodman, *Winnicott: Life and Work* (Cambridge, MA: Perseus Books, 2003).

even this first phase is already inflected by political concerns: what should we be striving for as a nation, if we want children to become capable of concern, reciprocity, and also happiness? Because Winnicott recognized (as many psychoanalysts do not) that the personal and the political are inseparable, he kept returning to political questions throughout his career. We'll examine this second phase further, but we must never forget that the two "phases" interpenetrate from the beginning. Even the ultimately happy Gabrielle was scarred by the Holocaust as well as by the birth of a new sibling.

Before we reach the second phase, however, we arrive at another terrifying discovery.

DEATH ENTERS THE MIND

At first, fear responds to hunger, thirst, darkness, wetness, and the helplessness of not being able to do anything about these bad things. As time goes on, a new idea enters the picture, an idea surely implicit in our evolutionary fear responses from the beginning: the idea of death. The infant is not aware of death, or of its own mortality. But its responses have evolved to serve survival, so we could say that in a sense, fear of hunger and thirst, even of the absence of comfort, is a fear of death. A vague fear of death may well be innate, an evolutionary advantage. And even the most loving parents transmit to young children their own fear of the "babacar," in times of family illness or political upheaval. So, we are preconditioned to avoid and fear mortality.

This innate or at least very early shrinking colors early fears. Even when a child has no explicit awareness of death, mortality colors the terror of childhood nightmares. The child fears a black emptiness, or a fall from an infinite height, or a devouring monster. When caretakers are gone, there is a terrible fear that they won't return—the source of babies' endless delight in games of disappearance and reappearance, as a loved toy, or the parent, vanishes suddenly, to reappear again to delighted giggles.

Gabrielle's nightmare fantasies clearly alluded to death: the "babacar," apparently taking her to annihilation; the devouring "black mother"; above all, the menacing "Sush baby," who threatened Gabrielle with extinction. Fear of loss of parental love and attention figured in her imagination as a kind of death. And why not? At that age she was unable to imagine a future of stability and the continuity of love. To a very young child, every temporary loss is a death. The central work of the three-year analysis with Winnicott was to produce trust: the sense that disruptions are not actually fatal, that teddy bears, analysts, and parents all survive and continue to love.

However well that lesson is learned, the child all too soon learns another darker one: that some animals and people do not reappear. Deaths of siblings and parents used to be routine events, and young children quickly learned to see the world, and their own existence, as a very fragile place. By the eighteenth century, Rousseau thought that his hypothetical pupil Emile might not see enough death to get the idea of his own vulnerability, so his imagined teacher begins talking about death by directing Emile to the deaths of small animals.[23]

As soon as children learn the idea of death, they pose many

[23]*Emile*, book IV.

questions, and they soon figure out that they themselves will die. Children react to this discovery in different ways, but always with a sense of deep dread and disturbance. When I was six—an anxious time for me, since my younger sister had just been born, and I felt that my parents were no longer interested in their former one and only—my grandmother took me to see Verdi's *Rigoletto* at the Metropolitan Opera. She had no interest in opera, and had no idea that anyone would be deeply moved by one, so she didn't recognize how odd her choice was. Seated in the third row of the orchestra, I was transfixed and traumatized. For weeks after that, I acted out with my dolls the concluding scene in which the dying Gilda (murdered by mistake because she has willingly taken the place of the fickle Duke, whom she loves) is handed to Rigoletto in a sealed sack. The jester looks inside, expecting to see the body of his hated enemy—and recoils with horror as he realizes that the sack actually contains his beloved child, about to breathe her last. I am sure the sack represented, to me, the mortal threat of my sister's birth and the way it took my breath away. But it also represented my budding awareness of my own mortality. The doll I put into the sack, when I reenacted the opera later, was Jo in my *Little Women* family of dolls, the one who represented me. When I opened the doll sack I was witnessing, and rehearsing, my own death. (I've been an opera fan ever since, and I believe that those powerful music-dramas are forms of Winnicottian play in which we deepen our insight, and even learn to breathe in the midst of tragedy.)

The fear of death has a lot to be said for it. It motivates us to pursue safety, health, and even peace. It moves us to shelter those we love, and to protect institutions and laws that we

love. Furthermore, when we recognize that we are mortal, this should remind us that we are profoundly equal. However much the kings and nobles of France might try to lord it over their subjects, they could not honestly deny that they were similar in the most important matter of all. That recognition might produce, as Rousseau devoutly hoped, compassion and reciprocity: we can band together to protect one another from hunger, disease, and war.

But the fear of death is also terrifying, and it envelops us always. Unlike other childhood fears it cannot be undone by reassurance. Parents who have left the room will return. New siblings do not remove parental love. We soon learn (sort of) that there is no monster in the closet, there is no witch who eats little children. But the fear of death is never false, and no learning can remove it. The babacar speeds onward into the darkness. Thus, fear persists beneath the fabric of daily life, producing good results, as Rousseau said. But it also leads to many strategies of narcissism, self-avoidance, and denial.

Lucretius claimed that the fear of death is the cause of all other fears in human life. This seems wrong. Life is just difficult, and it contains a lot to fear. Our human vulnerability itself is the source of fear, and only part of this fear is directed at death, since death is only one aspect of our vulnerability. The Greeks and Romans imagined gods who were immortal and who nonetheless could suffer many things: physical pain (Prometheus, his liver eaten eternally by a vulture), maiming (Uranus, castrated by his son, his testicles thrown into the sea), the loss of children (Zeus, mourning his dead son Sarpedon), and humiliation (Hera, betrayed countless times by her

husband). They knew, then, that immortality wouldn't remove fear. Still, Lucretius was probably right to think that the fear of death "suffuses" our lives with "the blackness of death," even if there is plenty of light and happiness around.

FEAR'S RHETORIC AND DEMOCRATIC ERROR

Fear makes us want to avoid disaster. But it certainly does not tell us how. In evolutionary prehistory, humans followed fear's instinctual prompting, fleeing predators and other deeply implanted dangers. In our complicated world, however, we can't rely on instinct, we have to think, and we had better think well. We need a conception of our well-being, and of what, and who, threatens it. In all societies this process of shaping fear is pervasively influenced by culture, politics, and rhetoric. Aristotle, remember, discussed fear in a treatise on rhetoric for future politicians. In order to persuade people to do what you want, he says, you have to understand how their emotions work, and then you can tailor what you say to their own psychology. Aristotle knew, of course, that people will use this advice for both good ends and bad.

Fear involves the thought of an imminent threat to our own well-being. Aristotle tells political speakers that they will be able to whip up fear only if (a) they portray the impending event as highly significant for survival or well-being, if (b) they make people think it is close at hand, and if, further (c) they make people feel that things are out of control—they can't ward off the bad thing easily on their own. They also have to

trust the speaker, he adds, so speakers must arrange to seem trustworthy.[24] Obviously, this advice will not always be used in the service of truth. Through our basic propensity to fear, democratic societies are highly vulnerable to manipulation.

The ancient Greek historian Thucydides tells a grim tale of democratic error.[25] The Athenians had voted to execute all the men of the rebellious colony of Mytilene, and to enslave the women and children. But they then calmed down and began to reconsider, reflecting on the terrible cruelty of condemning an entire city for a rebellion led by just a few—a crime that would likely count as genocide in modern terms. A demagogic orator named Cleon, who had initially proposed the vote for death, stepped forward to argue against any change of heart. Cleon, a fiery populist, made people both frightened and angry: this rebellion threatened Athenian safety, because all other colonies will rebel if they see they can get away with it. He portrayed the danger as imminent: Athenians will shortly have to risk their lives again and again.

Cleon prevailed. A ship was already on the way to carry out the lethal resolution. But then a different orator, Diodotus, stepped forward and, in a soothing and deliberate way, persuaded the assembly that their previous vote had indeed been wrong. People should not allow themselves to be stampeded by fear and anger: they should calmly consider their own future interests. There was no urgent danger, their safety was not really threatened by the rebellion, and it would be a serious

[24]On fear, see *Rhetoric* II.5, passim. On trustworthiness, *Rhetoric* I.2, 9.

[25]Thucydides, *History of the Peloponnesian War* (many translations), III.25–28, 35–50; the debate took place in 427 BCE.

error to commit acts of lethal aggression that would lose Athens the loyalty of many current allies.

The Athenians reversed their position and sent another ship to catch the first. By sheer luck, the first ship was becalmed, and the second one was able to catch up to it. By such a narrow thread hung thousands of lives. Even without deciding which speaker was correct, we can be sure one was wrong—and Thucydides makes it abundantly clear that he thinks Cleon is both wrong and, in his manipulative populist approach, a danger to the very survival of democracy at Athens. Fear can be manipulated by true and false information, producing both appropriate and inappropriate reactions.

How does error creep in? First, people have to have an idea of their own well-being and the well-being of society; there are many ways in which we can get this wrong. It's particularly easy to think too narrowly, equating social well-being with the well-being of our own group or class and forgetting the contributions of others. Cleon did this in a way that should strike us as familiar: by urging people to have a narrow view of Athenian supremacy that excludes allies and dependents. He "othered" the allies and made them all seem like potential enemies.

Even if people have an adequate conception of their welfare, they may be quite wrong about what really threatens it. The rebellion clearly insulted Athens, and Cleon got people to confuse insult with genuine risk. Some of these errors may be just a matter of getting the facts wrong; others may result from overestimation of some danger that is genuine, or the underestimation of other dangers (in this case, the danger of inspiring other defections from Athens by allies shocked at the

cruelty of her actions). People may also think themselves more vulnerable, and more helpless against the threat, than they really are.

Sometimes it seems that error is introduced by having too little fear. Athens made this error too, later, when it embarked on the disastrous Sicilian Expedition, refusing to heed sober advice. But what they should have heeded was not gusts or waves of fear, it was prudent calculation, facts, and evidence. And there's a good argument that even the grandiosity they exhibited in this rash act was an outgrowth of deeper fear. Lucretius says that wars of conquest are very often caused by a sense of powerlessness and basic vulnerability, which gives rise to the thought that if you extinguish all opposition, you will be safer. The rashness of the doomed expedition is not all that different from the rashness of murdering all the people of Mytilene—an unwise strategy of self-protection that takes the form of trying to eliminate all possible risks. It's not all that different from Proust's adult Marcel, who is driven mad with anxiety unless he pens Albertine up so that it is physically impossible for her to betray him.

FEAR'S LAWS: HEURISTICS AND BIASES

The new discipline of behavioral economics draws on psychological research to show us yet more about the errors of fear. Psychologists show that our assessments of risk are often inaccurate because, instead of soberly calculating costs and benefits, we use a number of heuristics that don't offer good guidance in today's complicated world, well though they may have guided us in evolutionary prehistory.[26]

One very common source of error in fear is what psychologists call "the availability heuristic": if a single type of problem is vivid in our experience, this leads us to overestimate the importance of the problem. This heuristic is a frequent problem in thought about environmental risks. People heard on the news that apples are contaminated by a dangerous pesticide, Alar—and this led many people to conclude, without further study, that the danger posed was huge. (The jury is still out on this one, but we certainly know by now that study, not panic, would have been the appropriate response. Alar remains classified as a probable carcinogen by the EPA, but the amount of the chemical that studies show potentially dangerous is extremely high, requiring an amount of Alar equal to that which one would ingest by drinking more than five thousand gallons of apple juice per day.) The availability heuristic also makes people fail to consider the full range of alternatives: for example, the fact that banning DDT will lead to an upsurge in deaths from malaria. In technical areas, there is no substitute for good and comprehensive scientific research, but the public often follows fear rather than science.

Another phenomenon that has been studied in the context of ethnic hostility is the "cascade": people respond to the behavior of other people by rushing to join them. Sometimes they join because of the reputation of those people—the "reputational

[26]One excellent source for these heuristics is Cass R. Sunstein, *Risk and Reason: Safety, Law, and the Environment* (Cambridge: Cambridge University Press, 2002), with further references to the psychological literature.

cascade"—and sometimes they join because they think that the behavior of others gives them new information—the "informational cascade." The economist Timur Kuran has argued that such cascades play a large role in the context of "ethnification," the shift (often amazingly rapid) in which people come to define themselves in terms of an ethnic or religious identity and to set themselves in opposition to some other ethnic group.[27] Psychoanalytic psychologist Sudhir Kakar, doing research on ethnic violence in India, independently arrives at a similar account.[28] Kakar's puzzle was why people who have lived together peacefully for years, Hindus and Muslims, suddenly turn hostile, defining their identity in a way they did not before, in terms of their religious ethnicity. His study shows that a large role is played by respected community leaders whose reputations produce unquestioning followers. A role is also played by the introduction of new "information" about danger allegedly posed by Muslims, often very unreliable.

Such tendencies threaten democracy in our nation today, as they have threatened India for many years. But there is a new development that makes things more volatile: social media and the Internet have made it easier for false reports to circulate and for cascades to develop. When a report "goes viral," emotions easily get out of control, in a way that is unlike the effect of newspaper reports, or even TV.

[27]Timur Kuran, "Ethnic Norms and Their Transformation Through Reputational Cascades," *Journal of Legal Studies* 27 (1998), 623–659, and see Sunstein, 37–39.

[28]Sudhir Kakar, *The Colors of Violence: Cultural Identities, Religion, and Conflict* (Chicago: University of Chicago Press, 1996).

What is the antidote to damaging informational cascades? Correct facts, informed public debate, and, most important, a spirit of dissent and independence on the part of citizens. Fear, however, always threatens the spirit of dissent. Fear makes people run for cover, seeking comfort in the embrace of a leader or a homogeneous group. Questioning feels naked and solitary.

In famous experiments, psychologist Solomon Asch showed that people have a surprisingly high level of submissiveness to peer pressure, even when the peers are saying things that are obviously false, such as which of two lines is longer (where the right answer is obvious).[29] People rationalized going along with such errors by saying that they were afraid to speak up. We're now in a position to understand the deep psychological forces involved. But, Asch also found, if even one person before the experimental subject did speak up and give the correct answer, this freed the subject to answer correctly. Dissent produces mental freedom from fear.

I'll have much more to say about the spirit of dissent, and how we might cultivate it. But we can see already that for dissent to do its job, people have to be willing to stand alone without crippling fear. The achievement of the child who learns to "play alone in the presence of its mother" must be paralleled by that of the adult who learns to argue alone in the presence of powerful forces of conformity. Democracy needs to cultivate that willingness to take risks for the truth and for good ideals. Americans grow up on valuable images of political

[29]Asch, "Opinions and Social Pressure" (1955), accessed at https://www.panarchy.org/asch/social.pressure.1955.html.

independence: Atticus Finch in *To Kill a Mockingbird*, the Henry Fonda character in *12 Angry Men*—and those American revolutionaries themselves, risking death to create the country we live in.

FEAR OF MUSLIMS: RHETORIC AND HEURISTICS, A TALE OF TWO PRESIDENTS

All the errors we have studied play a part in the crescendo of fear of Muslims that is such a prominent part of our national moment. Americans fear many things: loss of health care, expensive health care, Trump and his supporters, economic hardship, the success of women and minorities, racially biased police violence. To some extent each of these fears is both rational and useful; each, however, can get out of hand and disable sound thinking and cooperation. The fear of Muslims is a good place to apply what we have learned, seeing how a kernel of rational fear (fear of terrorist violence by criminals motivated by an extremist Islam-linked ideology) can escalate into fears that are irrational and harmful, producing a climate of mistrust that threatens to disable cherished democratic values. Fear is often manipulated by rhetoric, used by leaders who inspire their audience with trust.

The phenomenon is large and multiform. Let me take just one example of the rhetorical exploitation of fear to show where dangers kick in: President Trump's speech in Poland on June 11, 2017.

Some context first: The baseline ignorance of most Americans about Islam is huge. Most have no idea of the difference between Sunni and Shiite, and most have little sense of the national concentrations of Muslims in today's world: no idea, for example, that the two largest Muslim populations are in Indonesia and India, both thriving democracies. *Muslim* and *Arab* are often said, and thought, interchangeably. Nor are people aware, since few have read the Koran, that Islam at its inception was in essence a religion of equal respect, very much like Christianity—one reason why so many Indian Hindus from the lowest castes have converted to either one or the other. Americans have little sense of the different nations in which Muslims live, or of their histories and current struggles. Nor are they aware of differences of interpretation of the Koran, nor of the fact that the severe Wahhabi interpretation is popular today, to the extent that it is, largely because it has been supported by the rulers of Saudi Arabia, an American ally.

In this climate of ignorance, it is easy for all the mechanisms of fear I've identified to operate in a distorting way. First and most obviously, 9/11 and subsequent terrorist incidents involving Muslims become fertile ground for the "availability heuristic." These high-profile events blot out other sources of danger, stopping people from looking at such problems as easy access to guns without background checking, and leading them to support aggressive action in this one case, neglecting others, as if it were the best way to reduce vulnerability across the board.

A cousin of the availability heuristic that is always particularly damaging is a mental confusion between salience and proportional likelihood. We know this well in the area of race and criminal justice. If once African Americans get branded as criminals, on the basis of high-profile crimes committed by African Americans, then people often make two highly unreliable inferences: first, that a large proportion of crimes are committed by African Americans, and, second, that a large proportion of African Americans are criminals. Of course, even if the first were true, the second cannot be inferred from the first, and yet the regularity with which white people clutch their handbags or cross the street on seeing an African American shows how widespread such inferences are. Where Muslims are concerned, it's clear that people move much too rapidly from salient terrorist incidents to an idea that most terrorist incidents are committed by Muslims, a claim that can't easily be studied well, since the definition of *terrorism* is so vague and disputed. And then, the far more serious mental error, they move from the idea that most terrorist acts are caused by Muslims to the conclusion that most Muslims are terrorists or potential terrorists, a claim that is both glaringly false and highly counterproductive, since one good way to get information about possible Islamic terrorist acts is to cultivate good relations with the local Muslim community.

Cascades, both reputational and informational, play a huge role in stoking these generalized fears. The Internet makes cascades easy. Just as cute cat videos harmlessly go viral, so damaging and misleading information spreads rapidly, often further boosted by the Internet reputation of some commentator or self-proclaimed authority.

Further feeding fear are likely innate neurological mechanisms. Just as we are apparently hardwired to fear the shape of the snake, so we seem to be hardwired to fear a person who is hidden, whose face cannot be seen. Horror movies know this well. Just as Darth Vader is scary precisely because his human voice issues forth from a mask and a full-body covering, so to, to many Americans at least, Muslim women in full covering inspire fear, particularly when the face is covered. Although our deep respect for religious choices has kept the United States from following some European countries that have actually banned the burqa, there's no doubt that it does inspire many people with unease and vague alarm—even though in the US and Europe, there is virtually no evidence of terrorist acts committed by women, and even though deliberate terrorists such as the Boston Marathon bombers try hard to blend in: those two wore baseball caps and T-shirts and carried backpacks. It's notable, too, that people do not shrink from lots of other types of full-body and even facial covering, such as normal winter attire (long down coat, hat pulled down over the eyebrows, scarf over mouth and nose, opaque or reflecting sunglasses), or the uniforms of winter athletes, surgeons, dentists, people attending a costume party. (Indeed, the French law banning facial covering had to include a long list of exceptions, including reasons of "health," "sport," "profession," and "artistic and cultural events.")

Despite the clear evidence of unevenness and clannishness in American and European fears, an innate aversion to the covered face, *when combined with* our innate clannish aversion to anything strange and unfamiliar, makes many Americans shrink from Muslims in a way that people don't shrink from more familiar-looking members of groups some of whose members engage in violence. For example, people never shrank from people known to be Irish Catholics, or proposed to limit

Irish Catholic immigration—despite the fact that Northern Ireland's "troubles" have generated a very large number of terrorist acts, and that most of the money supporting IRA (Irish Republican Army) terrorism came from the US. Even in Britain, where most of the terrorist acts took place, people didn't generally shun the Irish (they understood that the Republic and Northern Ireland were totally different entities), nor did they generally shun Roman Catholics, although the IRA was a Catholic terrorist organization. Nor did anyone try to invoke the idea of a "clash of civilizations," which would have been absurd, given that all parties were white and Christian. In short, they followed the evidence and rarely succumbed to irresponsible fear—no doubt because all parties were white and Christian.

Above all, fear responds to rhetoric, as Aristotle knew long ago. And our two most recent Republican presidents have handled the job of public communication very differently. After 9/11, Americans were insistently told by President George W. Bush that we are not at war with Islam. "We are not at war with Islam," he famously said. And he didn't say it just once: he kept on repeating that message frequently, as one can see by reading the archive at https://georgewbush-whitehouse.archives.gov/infocus/ramadan/islam.html. Some representative examples:

On December 5, 2002, at the Islamic Center of Washington, DC:

> "Here in the United States our Muslim citizens are making many contributions in business, science and law, medicine and education, and in other fields. Muslim members of our Armed Forces and of my administration are serving their

> fellow Americans with distinction, upholding our nation's ideals of liberty and justice in a world at peace."

On November 13, 2002, at a meeting with UN Secretary General Kofi Annan:

> "Some of the comments that have been uttered about Islam do not reflect the sentiments of my government or the sentiments of most Americans. Islam, as practiced by the vast majority of people, is a peaceful religion, a religion that respects others. Ours is a country based upon tolerance and we welcome people of all faiths in America."

On November 20, 2002, at a press conference:

> "Ours is a war not against a religion, not against the Muslim faith. But ours is a war against individuals who absolutely hate what America stands for . . ."

There's a lot more in this archive, and the very fact that President Bush kept such an archive is itself significant. For me, this is how a responsible leader reacts in the face of widespread popular fear. He calms escalating confusion and anxiety, leading people toward a more fact-based and pinpointed strategy, and reminding them of cherished American values that must not be sacrificed. (More questionable, admittedly, was the famous "Axis of Evil" speech of January 29, 2002, in which President Bush did demonize a group of nations thought to sponsor terrorism: but at least the focus was on state-sponsored criminal activity rather than on the entirety of a religion, and indeed the inclusion of North Korea made it clear that he did not consider state-sponsored terrorism a peculiarly Islamic phenomenon.)

More generally, President Bush typically used the rhetoric of universal human dignity and progress, rather than the rhetoric of a clash of "civilizations." For example, he urged the US and Europe to "help men and women around the world to build lives of purpose and dignity," and to "protect the health of the world's people." This rhetoric was also valuable, calming inaccurate fear and getting people to focus narrowly on evidence of real danger, while engaging in constructive policies, helpful to human life around the world. (Such statements are of a piece with President Bush's insistence that the pharmaceutical companies provide anti-retroviral drugs at a reasonable price in Africa.)

President Trump, by contrast, both during his campaign and after it, has repeatedly alluded to Islam as if it were, as a whole, a source of danger. The rhetoric preceding the controversial travel ban singled out Muslims as potential enemies, often using the words *Muslim ban*. The speech he gave in Warsaw on July 6, 2017, which was widely praised, seems almost more ominous because more subtle. The speech asks whether "the West" still has the will to fight against an enemy that is portrayed as monolithic and evil. From a description of Poland's "fight . . . for freedom" against the Nazis (whom the speech oddly conflated with the Soviets, who were of course our allies!), the speech segues rapidly to a current threat: "another oppressive ideology" that "seeks to export terrorism and extremism all around the globe." Although the threat is named "radical Islamic terrorism," not Islam as such, and although the president alludes to his request to "the leaders of more than fifty Muslim nations to join together to drive out this menace which threatens all of humanity," the speech nonetheless subscribes to the old familiar "clash of civilizations" idea. As Peter Beinart notes in *The Atlantic* on July 6, the speech refers ten times to "the West" and five times to "our civilization."[30] The thesis of Samuel Huntington to which this rhetoric alludes is that "the West" is at war with Islamic civilization as a whole.[31]

And what is "the West"? It is not a geographical entity, since it includes Australia and Poland and excludes nations such as Egypt and Morocco that are further west than some of the included nations. And, as Beinart notes, it is not a political or economic term either, since Japan, South Korea, and India are not included. Basically, it is an appeal to shared religion and shared racial identity: to Christianity (with some Jews included) and to whiteness (since Latin America does not appear to be included).

[30]Peter Beinart, "The Racial and Religious Paranoia of Trump's Warsaw Speech," *The Atlantic*, July 6, 2017, https://www.theatlantic.com/international/archive/2017/07/trump-speech-poland/532866/.

[31]Samuel P. Huntington, *The Clash of Civilizations and the Remaking of World Order* (New York: Simon & Schuster, 1996). One remarkable oddity of Huntington's view of history is that India is said to have a uniformly Hindu "civilization," and not even to be one of the "split" countries—ignoring the profound intermingling and interpenetration of Hinduism and Islam throughout long stretches of Indian history.

As political analysis, the speech makes no sense. The Islamic world is at war within itself, and there is no single organization or group, among the many mutually hostile groups, that has the power to threaten a military invasion of even the weakest European nation. The speech is not about analysis, however; it is about stoking fear of the "south" and "east," or, more precisely, of immigrants from those regions. Beinart's conclusion seems to me correct: in Trump's view, "America is at its core Western: meaning white and Christian (or at least Judeo-Christian). The implication is that anyone in the United States who is not white and Christian may not truly be American but rather an imposter and a threat."

The president's rhetoric, unlike the rhetoric of President Bush, creates a demon without directing attention to crucial facts. it stokes fear by creating a sense of a large and unbounded danger (the south, the east), and of imminence and urgency. It then segues into the rhetoric of blame and self-defense, as fear stokes anger. I'll follow this connection in my next chapter.

In short, fear of Muslims today draws on all the mechanisms of fear I have discussed: innate tendencies, deeply embedded psychological heuristics, and people's responsiveness to political rhetoric. This type of amorphous fear, generated in a climate of ignorance and fed by imprecise and alarmist rhetoric, is the enemy of any sane dialogue about our future. Fortunately, good analysts know how to dissent.

This is just one example of American fear gone awry. The same type of analysis should be carried out with other fears, too: What are people thinking and picturing? Why? How well focused is the fear, and how well supported with correct information? To the extent that the fear is narrowly targeted, has one instance been overemphasized to the neglect of others equally serious? If a fear is well grounded and balanced, and yet there is a danger that people will ignore the problem and fail to act, some hype can be warranted, as when a politician trying to get citizens to evacuate calls an oncoming hurricane a "monster storm." But even well-grounded exaggeration should be indulged only with great caution.

THE FACILITATING ENVIRONMENT, PART II

We are vulnerable, and our lives are prone to fear. Even in times of happiness and success, fear nibbles around the edges of concern and reciprocity, turning us away from others and toward a narcissistic preoccupation with ourselves. Fear is monarchical, and democratic reciprocity a hard-won achievement.

Winnicott, optimistic despite taking the full measure of these dangers, thought that people could attain "mature interdependence" if they had a "facilitating environment," and he thought that this environment was often attained. Given his profession, his focus throughout his life was on attaining it in the individual child's life in the family. Many children already had such an environment; if they did not, one could be supplied by the patient work of the analyst. But his wartime work led him to speculate about the larger question: what would it be like for society as a whole to be a "facilitating environment" for the cultivation of its people and their human relationships?

Such a society, he thought (as the Cold War advanced) would have to be a freedom-protecting democracy, since only that form of society fully and equally nourished people's capacities to grow, play, act, and express themselves.[32] He repeatedly connected democracy with psychic health: to live with others on terms of mutual interdependence and equality, people have to transcend the narcissism in which we all start life. We have to renounce the wish to enslave others, substituting concern, goodwill, and the acceptance of limits for infantile aggression.

We have a vague idea of what these goals mean in the family, and Winnicott always emphasized that a key job of government was to support families, though he said little about this in a practical way. We can certainly see, ourselves, that families cannot make children secure and balanced, capable of withstanding onslaughts of fear, if they are hungry, if they lack medical care, if children lack good schools and a safe neighborhood environment. This leads us to the larger question that Winnicott only vaguely addressed: how can a nation be, as a whole, a "facilitating environment" that allays fear and protects democratic reciprocity?

It's an urgent question, and the stakes are high. Because this is not a book of detailed public policy, I won't even attempt solutions to these problems here, although in chapter 7 I shall propose general strategies. For now, let's summarize the problem as it emerges from my analysis. Fear always simmers beneath the surface of moral concern, and it threatens to destabilize

[32]See especially "Some Thoughts on the Meaning of the Word Democracy," in *The Family and Individual Development*.

democracy, since democracy requires all of us to limit our narcissism and embrace reciprocity. Right now, fear is running rampant in our nation: fear of declining living standards, fear of unemployment, of the absence of health care in time of need; fear of an end to the American Dream, in which you can be confident that hard work brings a decent and stable life and that your children will do better than you did if they, too, work hard.

Our narrative of fear tells us that some very bad things can easily happen. Citizens may become indifferent to truth and prefer the comfort of an insulating peer group who repeat one another's falsehoods. They may become afraid of speaking out, preferring the comfort of a leader who gives them a womb-like feeling of safety. And they may become aggressive against others, blaming them for the pain of fear. To this fear-blame dynamic we now turn.

3

ANGER, CHILD OF FEAR

America is an angry country. That's an old story, but today the anger seems more ubiquitous and more strident. Men blame women, women blame working-class men. On the right we find hysterical blame of Muslims, on the left furious blame of those who denounce Muslims. Immigrants blame the new political regime for the instability of their lives. Dominant groups blame immigrants for the instability of "all our" lives. Truth matters, of course, and I shall insist on that. Still, the blaming we see is, all too often, not measured but hysterical, fear-driven, refusing calm deliberation. And it is retributive, seeking to inflict pain in return for the pain the angry person or group is suffering. Public anger contains not just protest at wrongs, a reaction that is healthy for democracy when the protest is well grounded, but also a burning desire for payback, as if the suffering of someone else could solve the group's or the nation's problems.

We could try to understand this anger by thinking harder about our own political moment. But, especially where anger is concerned, I believe that we rarely think clearly when we are thinking about ourselves and our own immediate time. We do better, I think, to turn first to the past, looking at the issue through the lens of historical and literary examples that we can discuss together without partisan defensiveness. So, I propose to turn first to ancient Greece and Rome, where there is much that speaks to the issues of our day. Let's ponder the ending of one of the most famous Greek tragedies, the *Oresteia* of Aeschylus (458 BCE) which explores the curse of retributive anger that haunted the house of Atreus—and the political resolution of that curse, through political democracy and the rule of law. Although ostensibly set in remote mythic times, the trilogy culminates in a praise of fifth-century Athenian institutions, and its third play, *Eumenides*, is full of anachronistic references to the system of criminal law with which the audience would be familiar.[1]

At the end of the *Oresteia*, then, two transformations take place in the city of Athens. One is famous, the other often neglected. In the famous transformation, Athena introduces legal institutions to replace and terminate the cycle of blood

[1]I also discuss the *Oresteia* in *Anger and Forgiveness: Resentment, Generosity, Justice* (New York: Oxford, 2016), ch. 1, but I've changed some nuances of my interpretation. Here I use the Greek text and translate myself, but for those who want a good translation to read, I recommend Richmond Lattimore's for its poetic qualities, that of Hugh Lloyd-Jones for literal accuracy.

vengeance. Setting up a court of law with established procedures of evidence and argument, and a jury selected by lot from the citizen body of Athens, she announces that blood guilt will now be settled by law, rather than by the Furies, ancient goddesses of revenge. But the Furies are not simply dismissed. Instead, Athena persuades them to join the city, giving them a place of honor beneath the earth, in recognition of their importance for the health of the city.

Typically, Athena's move is understood to be a recognition that the legal system must incorporate and honor the retributive passions. These passions themselves remain unchanged; they simply have a new house built around them. The Furies agree to accept the constraints of law, but they retain an unchanged nature, dark and vindictive.

That reading, however, ignores the second transformation, a transformation in the character of the Furies themselves. As the drama begins, the Furies are described as repulsive and horrifying. They are said to be black, disgusting; their eyes drip a hideous liquid. Apollo even says they vomit up clots of blood that they have ingested from their prey. They belong, he says, in some barbarian tyranny where cruelty reigns.

Nor, when they awaken, do the Furies give the lie to these grim descriptions. As the ghost of the murdered Clytemnestra calls them, they do not speak, but simply make animal noises, moaning and whining. (The Greek says *mugmos* and *oigmos*, animal noises.) When they do begin to speak, their only words are "get him get him get him get him," as close to a predator's hunting cry as the genre allows. As Clytemnestra says: "In your dream you pursue your prey, and you bark like a hunting dog hot on the trail of blood." If the Furies are later given poetic speech, as the genre demands, we are never to forget this initial characterization.

What Aeschylus has done is to depict unbridled resentment. It is obsessive, destructive, existing only to inflict pain and ill. (As the distinguished eighteenth-century philosopher Bishop Butler observes, "No other principle, or passion, hath for its end the misery of our fellow creatures.") Apollo's idea is that this rabid breed belongs somewhere else, surely not in a law-abiding democracy.

Unchanged, these Furies could not be at the foundation of a legal system in a society committed to the rule of law. You don't put wild dogs in a cage and come out with justice. But the Furies do not make the transition to democracy unchanged. Until quite late in the drama, they are still their bestial selves, threatening to disgorge their venom on the land. Then, however, Athena persuades them to alter themselves so as to join her enterprise. "Lull to repose the bitter force of your black wave of anger," she tells them. But, of course, that means a virtual change of identity, so bound up are they with anger's obsessive force. She offers them incentives to join the democracy: a place of honor, reverence from the citizens—but only if they adopt a new range of sentiments, substituting future-directed benevolence for retribution. Perhaps most fundamental of all, they must listen to the voice of persuasion. They accept her offer and express themselves "with gentle-tempered intent." Each, they declare, should give generously to each, in a "mind-set of common love." Not surprisingly, they are transformed physically in related ways. They apparently assume an erect posture for the procession that concludes the drama, and they receive crimson robes from a group of citizen escorts. They have become Athenians, rather than beasts. Their very name is changed: they are now The Kindly Ones (Eumenides), not The Furies.

This second transformation is just as significant as the first one, indeed crucial to the success of the first one. Aeschylus shows that a democratic legal order can't just put a cage around retribution; it must fundamentally transform it from something hardly human, obsessive, bloodthirsty, to something human, accepting of reasons, something that protects life rather than threatening it. The Furies are still needed, because this is an imperfect world and there are always crimes to be dealt with. But they are not wanted or needed in their original form. They must become instruments of justice and human welfare. The city is liberated from the scourge of vindictive anger, which produces civil strife. In its place, the city gets forward-looking justice.

Like modern democracies, the ancient Greek democracy had an anger problem. Read the historians and the speeches of the orators, and you will see some things that are not remote: individuals litigating obsessively against people they blame for having wronged them; groups blaming other groups for their lack of power; citizens blaming prominent politicians and other elites for selling out the dearest values of the democracy; other groups blaming foreign visitors, or even women, for their own political and personal woes.

The anger that the Greeks—and, later, the Romans—knew all too well, was an anger full of fear at one's own human vulnerability. Lucretius even says that all political anger is an outgrowth of fear—of infantile helplessness and its adult cousin the fear of death. Fear, he says, makes everything worse, leading to political ills to which we'll return. For now, however, let's focus on anger.

The Greeks and Romans saw a lot of anger around them. But as classical scholar William Harris shows in his fine book *Restraining Rage*,[2] they did not embrace or valorize anger. They did not define manliness in terms of anger, and indeed, as with those Furies, tended to impute it to women, whom they saw as lacking rationality. However much they felt and expressed anger, they waged a cultural struggle against it, seeing it as destructive of human well-being and democratic institutions. The first word of Homer's *Iliad* is *anger*—the anger of Achilles that "brought thousandfold pains upon the Achaeans." And the *Iliad*'s hopeful ending requires Achilles to give up his anger and to be reconciled with his enemy Priam, as both acknowledge the frailty of human life.

I'll try to convince you that the Greeks and Romans are right: anger is a poison to democratic politics, and it is all the worse when fueled by a lurking fear and a sense of helplessness. I worked on anger in my 2016 book *Anger and Forgiveness*,[3] but I now feel that the analysis there left out something crucial: the role of fear as both source and accomplice of retributive anger. I'll try to convince you that we should resist anger in ourselves and inhibit its role in our political culture.

[2]William Harris, *Restraining Rage: The Ideology of Anger Control in Classical Antiquity* (Cambridge, MA: Harvard University Press, 2002).
[3]Above, n. 1.

That idea, however, is radical and evokes strong opposition. For anger, with all its ugliness, is a popular emotion. Many people think that it is impossible to care for justice without anger at injustice, and that anger should be encouraged as part of a transformative process. Many also believe that it is impossible for individuals to stand up for their own self-respect without anger, that someone who reacts to wrongs and insults without anger is spineless and downtrodden. Nor are these ideas confined to the sphere of personal relations. The most popular position in the sphere of criminal justice today is "retributivism," the view that the law ought to punish aggressors in a manner that embodies the spirit of justified anger seeking to inflict retributive pain. And it is also very widely believed that successful challenges against great injustice need that type of anger to make progress.

Still, we may persist in our Aeschylean skepticism, remembering that recent years have seen three noble and successful freedom movements conducted in a spirit of non-anger: those of Mohandas Gandhi, Martin Luther King Jr., and Nelson Mandela—surely people who stood up for their self-respect and that of others, and who did not acquiesce in injustice.

I'll now argue that a philosophical analysis of anger can help us support these philosophies of non-anger, showing why retributive anger is fatally flawed from a normative viewpoint—sometimes incoherent, sometimes based on bad values, and especially poisonous when people use it to deflect attention from real problems that they feel powerless to solve. Anger pollutes democratic politics and is of dubious value in both life and the law. I'll present my general view, and then show its relevance to thinking well about the struggle for political justice, taking our ongoing struggle for racial justice as my example.

THE ROOTS OF ANGER: RAGE, IDEAS OF UNFAIRNESS

Let's now return briefly to that helpless fearful baby whom Lucretius brilliantly described. Babies at birth don't have anger as such, because full-fledged anger requires causal thinking: someone did something bad to me. Babies yell when they don't get what they want, and the yell, at first, expresses discomfort rather than blame—because the child can't think about causation.

Fairly soon, however, a further idea creeps in: those caretakers are not giving me what I desperately need. They did this to me. It's because of them that I am cold, wet, and hungry. Experiences of being fed, held, and clothed quickly lead to expectations, expectations to demands. Instinctual self-love makes us value our own survival and comfort. But the self is threatened by others, when they don't do what we want and expect. Psychoanalyst Melanie Klein refers to this emotional reaction in infants as "persecutory anxiety," since it is indeed fear, but coupled with an idea of a vague threat coming from outside.[4] I would prefer to call it fear-anger or even fear-blame.

If we were not helpless, we would just go get what we need. But since we are initially helpless, we have to rely on others.

[4]Klein's writings on this topic are voluminous. A good summary, with references, can be found at http://www.melanie-klein-trust.org.uk/paranoid-schizoid-position.

They don't always give us what we need, and then, once we can identify the "culprit," we lash out, blaming them. Blame gives us a strategy: now I'll enforce my will by raging and making noise. But it also expresses an underlying picture of the world: the world ought to give us what we demand. When people don't do that, they are bad.

Protest and blame are positive, in a sense: they construct an orderly purposive world in which I am an agent, making demands. My life is valuable, things ought to be arranged so that I am happy and my needs are met. That hasn't happened, so someone must be blamed. But a retributive idea all too often infects the thought of blame, and often even of punishment: the people we blame ought to suffer for what they have done. Psychologist Paul Bloom has shown that retributive thinking appears very early in the lives of infants, even before they begin to use language. Infants are delighted when they see the "bad person"—a puppet who has snatched something from another puppet—beaten with a stick. Bloom calls this an early sense of justice.[5] I prefer to call it the internal Furies that inhabit us all and that are not securely linked to real justice. The infants' idea looks like a version of the *lex talionis*: an eye for an eye, pain for pain. It's likely that this crude idea of proportional payback has an evolutionary origin. It is a leap to call this an idea of justice, and I think we should not make this leap.

Notice that infantile anger rests on a profound contradiction, within which most of human life is lived. On the one

[5]Paul Bloom, *Just Babies: The Origins of Good and Evil* (New York: Crown, 2013).

hand, I am helpless, and the universe doesn't care about me. On the other hand, I am a monarch, and everyone must care about me. The combination of physical helplessness with evolutionary self-love and infantile narcissism produces that contradiction, which, as we'll see, typically persists throughout life in the form of crude "just world" thinking and a tendency to blame others for life's hardships and misfortunes.

DEFINING ANGER

Let's now fast-forward to human adulthood. People now experience and express not just infantile anger, but full-fledged anger. But what is anger? As I said, philosophers like definitions, which are useful to clear our heads, in this case helping us separate the potentially promising parts of anger from those that lead to nothing but trouble. And, back to the Greeks, let's talk about Aristotle's definition, since more or less all the definitions of anger in the Western philosophical tradition are modeled on it.[6] (Those in Indian traditions—unfortunately the only non-Western traditions known to me—are very similar.[7])

According to Aristotle, anger is a response to a significant damage to something or someone one cares about, and a damage that the angry person believes to have been wrongfully inflicted. Aristotle adds that although anger is painful, it also contains within itself a pleasant hope for payback or

[6]Aristotle's definition is in his *Rhetoric*, book II, ch. 2, which also discusses how to stir up anger; chapter 3 discusses how to remove anger.
[7]See especially the discussion of Indian Buddhist philosopher Santideva in my *Anger and Forgiveness.*

retribution. So: *significant damage*, pertaining to one's own values or circle of cares, and *wrongfulness*. Those two elements seem both true and uncontroversial, and they have been validated by modern psychological studies. Those parts of anger can go wrong in specific and local ways: we might be wrong about who did the bad thing, or how significant it was, or whether it was done wrongfully (rather than accidentally). But they are often on target.

More controversial, certainly, is the idea that the angry person wants some type of retribution, and that this is a conceptual part of what anger is. All the Western philosophers who talk about anger include this wish as a conceptual element in anger.[8] Still, we need to pause, since it is not obvious. We should understand that the wish for retribution can be a very subtle wish: the angry person doesn't need to wish to take revenge herself. She may want the law to punish the wrongdoer; or even some type of divine justice. Or, she may, more subtly, simply want the wrongdoer's life to go badly in the future—hoping, for example, that the second marriage of her betraying spouse is a dismal failure. I think if we understand the wish in this broad way, Aristotle is right: anger typically does contain a sort of strike-back tendency, and that is what differentiates it from compassionate grieving. Contemporary psychologists who study anger empirically agree with Aristotle in seeing this double movement in it, from pain to hope.[9]

[8]Thus, the Greek and Roman Stoics, who categorize all emotions around two dimensions—present/future, and good/bad, classify anger in the "good-future" category, not in "present-bad."

[9]See, for example, Carol Tavris, *Anger: The Misunderstood Emotion* (New

We should understand, however, that the two parts of anger can come apart. We can feel outrage at the wrongfulness of an act or an unjust state of affairs, without wanting payback for the wrong done to us. I'll be arguing that the outrage part is personally and socially valuable when our beliefs are correct: we need to recognize wrongful acts and protest them, expressing our concern for the violation of an important norm. And there is one species of anger, I believe, that is free of the retributive wish: its entire content is "How outrageous that is. Something must be done about that." I call this "Transition-Anger," because it expresses a protest, but faces forward: it gets to work finding solutions rather than dwelling on the infliction of retrospective pain. (The ordinary word *indignation* is often used to refer to this type of anger, but usage is inconstant, so I prefer the made-up term.)

Take parents and children. Parents often feel that children have acted wrongfully, and they are outraged. They want to protest the wrong, and somehow to hold the child accountable. But they usually avoid retributive payback. They rarely think (today at least), "Now you have to suffer for what you have done," as if that by itself was a fitting response. Instead, they ask themselves what sort of reaction will produce future improvement in the child. Usually this will not be a painful payback, and it certainly won't obey the *lex talionis*, "an eye for an eye." If their child hits a playmate, parents do not hit their child as if that were "what you deserve." Instead, they choose

---

York: Simon & Schuster, 1982, revised edition 1989); other references are given in *Anger and Forgiveness*.

strategies that are firm enough to get the child's attention and that express clearly that and how what the child did was wrong. And they give positive suggestions for the future, how to do things differently. So, loving parents typically have the outrage part of anger without the payback part—where their children are concerned, because they love them. This will be a clue to my positive proposal for democratic society, where I fear we do not always love our fellow citizens.

Nor is this constructive response peculiar to asymmetrical relations of care. Think of a good friendship. In any friendship there are slights and errors. One friend feels hurt by what the other has done. Still, if it's a strong friendship, the hurt friend won't even think of inflicting pain for pain. She will probably tell the friend what seems wrong to her, expressing her sense of what important values the friend's conduct has shortchanged. But then she will do whatever seems likely to enlist the other friend's cooperation going forward, mending the breach, and preventing further errors.

Retributive wishes, however, are a deep part of human nature, fostered by some parts of the major religions and by many societal cultures, although they have been denounced by religious and social radicals from Jesus and the Buddha to Mohandas Gandhi.[10] They may have served us well in a pre-social condition, deterring aggression. But the idea that pain is made good or assuaged by pain, however widespread, is a deceptive fiction. Killing the killer does not restore the dead to life, although the demand for capital punishment is endorsed

[10]See *Anger and Forgiveness*, ch. 3 for discussion.

by many families of victims as if it did somehow set things to rights. Pain for pain is an easy idea: even Bloom's babies have it. But it is a false lure, creating more pain instead of rectifying the problem. As Gandhi is reported to have said, "An eye for an eye makes the whole world blind."

This wish for payback arises in all sorts of situations. Take divorce. Betrayed spouses often feel entitled to seek punitive divorce settlements and child custody arrangements, as if that somehow were their due, and as if punitive payback somehow restored the balance of power or rescued their damaged dignity. But in real life the function of payback is usually far less benign. Two people become locked in a struggle for pain, focused on the past, and often inflicting great collateral damage on children, friends, and family. In the end, the betrayer may get "his comeuppance," but what does that achieve? Typically, it does not improve the litigant's life going forward. By focusing obsessively on the past, she becomes closed to new possibilities, and she often becomes bitter and unpleasant. What the payback seeker wants is future happiness and self-respect. Payback by itself never achieves that, and it usually makes the world a lot worse for all.

Or take that friendship I imagined. Suppose the hurt friend thinks, *I'll hurt you back, and that will balance things out and make everything all right.* Many people think this way. But such people don't make good friends. The retributive hurting is likely to make things worse, perhaps damaging the friendship beyond repair.

Retaliation feels manly and strong to many Americans (male and female): a real man (a strong woman) will strike back against an injury to himself or his own. Not all cultures have thought this way. The ancient Greeks and Romans thought that anger was a sign of weakness, and either childish or "womanish," since they thought women were weak creatures. Strength, they thought, means not getting drawn into the "blood for blood" game. In ancient mythology, retribution is ugly, as the ancient Greek tragic poet Aeschylus illustrated by depicting the Furies, goddesses of revenge, as foul, poisonous to politics because they were unable to think about human well-being.

But wait a minute. We all agree that wrongful acts, if they are serious enough, should be punished, and punishment is typically painful. Yes, we should agree that punishment is often useful: but why and how? We might see punishment in a retributive spirit, as payback for what has already happened. That is the attitude I have been criticizing, and it does great social harm, leading to a gruesome pile-on-the-misery strategy, as if it really compensated for the damages of crime. But there's a better attitude, more like that of the good parent in my example: we might try to look to the future and produce a better society, using punishment to express the value we attach to human life and safety, to deter other people from committing that crime, and, we hope, to deter that individual from committing another crime, or at least incapacitating him. In some cases, reform is a further possibility to be explored.

If we think this way, however, trying to improve the future, we probably will have a lot of other thoughts before we get to punishment. Like that good parent, we will think that people don't do wrong nearly as often, if they are basically loved and respected, if they have enough to eat, if they get a decent education, if they are healthy, and if they foresee a future of opportunity. So, thinking about crime will lead us in the direction of designing a society in which people have fewer incentives to commit crime. When they do, despite our best efforts, we take that seriously, for the sake of the future.[11]

There is one more part to Aristotle's definition. He says that anger is always a response not to any old damage, but only to the type he calls a "down-ranking." This does not seem to be true all the time. I can get angry at wrongs done to others, without thinking of them as a down-ranking of myself. Later philosophers hold on to the other parts of Aristotle's definition but drop this restriction: anger can be a response to any wrongful act, not just a status injury. Still, let's hold on to Aristotle's idea, for it does cover surprisingly many cases of anger, as empirical researchers emphasize.

The status idea is important because it is the one case, I believe, where payback gives you what you want. If what you are focused on is not the murder, or theft, or rape itself, but only the way it has affected your *relative* status in the world, then by pushing the wrongdoer relatively lower, you really do push yourself relatively higher. And if relative status is all you care about, you needn't be worried that the underlying harms caused by the wrongful act (murder, rape, theft) have not been made good. If you're thinking only about relative status, then,

[11]This was the view of all the major Greek and Roman philosophers, but it did not become prominent again in the Judeo-Christian West until the eighteenth century, with the criminal law reform proposals of Cesare Beccaria and Jeremy Bentham.

payback sort of makes sense. Many people think this way, and that may help explain why payback is so popular and why people do not quickly conclude that it is an empty diversion from the task of fixing the future.

What is wrong with the status idea? Focus on relative status was common in ancient Greece: indeed, it explains Achilles's anger when Agamemnon insults him by taking "his" woman away. Focus on status was common, too, at the founding of the United States, as Lin-Manuel Miranda's brilliant *Hamilton* reminds us all. Elaborate codes of honor and status led, indeed, to constant status-anxiety and to many duels responding to purported insults.[12]

What's wrong with the obsession with status is that life is not all about reputation; it is about more substantial things: love, justice, work, family. We all know people today who are obsessed with what other people think of them, who constantly scan the Internet to see who has been insulting them. Social media may encourage this obsession, as people diss each other, count the number of "likes" some post of theirs has garnered, and so forth. As we live more and more in the eyes of others, more and more of our lives come in for rating, up or down. But isn't this obsession with status a sign of insecurity? And doesn't it increase insecurity, since that person who scans the world for signs of disfavor is certain to find some? Equally important, isn't the obsession with status a diversion from more important values? Achilles had to learn how bad it was

[12]See Joanne Freeman, *Affairs of Honor: National Politics in the New Republic* (New Haven: Yale University Press, 2002).

to destroy thousands of people on account of one insult; Aaron Burr never learned much, it appears, but his example shows us what we forfeit when we become obsessed with being "in the room where it happens."

Notice that obsession with relative status is different from a focus on human dignity or self-respect, since dignity belongs to everyone, and people are equal in dignity (at least this is how we ought to think and usually do think), so dignity does not establish a hierarchy, and nobody would be tempted to suppose that inflicting humiliation on someone else would boost my human dignity. Dignity, unlike reputation, is equal and inalienable.[13]

THREE ERRORS IN ANGER

We're now ready to see three ways anger cans lead us astray.

1. THE OBVIOUS ERRORS. Anger can be misguided, and guide us badly, if it is based on wrong information about who did what to whom, about whether the bad act was really done wrongfully (with some sort of bad intent) rather than just by

[13]Political philosophers have defended many different views of human dignity, and many have based it on the possession of rationality or some other characteristic thought to belong only to humans. My view allows the ascription of full and equal dignity to humans with severe cognitive impairments and also, a different topic not for the present book, to most non-human animals. See my *Frontiers of Justice: Disability, Nationality, Species Membership* (Cambridge, MA: Harvard University Press, 2006), and "Human Dignity and Political Entitlements," in *Human Dignity and Bioethics: Essays Commissioned by the President's Council on Bioethics* (Washington, DC: 2008), 351–380.

accident, and also if it is based on a confused sense of importance. Aristotle mentions people who get angry when someone forgets their name, and this familiar example is a case of overestimating the importance of what the person did. (Probably also a case of getting intention wrong.) Since we're often hasty when we are angry, these errors occur often.

2. THE STATUS ERROR. We also go wrong, I claim, if we think relative status is hugely important and focus on that to the exclusion of other things. This error is really a case of mistaking the importance of a particular value, but since it is so common and such a major source of anger, we have to single it out and give it a separate number.
3. THE PAYBACK ERROR. Finally, we very often go wrong when we permit deeply ingrained retributive thoughts to take over, making us think that pain wipes out pain, death murder, and so forth. In short, when we think that inflicting pain in the present fixes the past. We go wrong because that thought is a kind of irrational magical thinking, and because it distracts us from the future, which we can change, and often should.

THE FOURTH ERROR IN ANGER: HELPLESSNESS AND THE "JUST WORLD"

All these errors are common, not least in the political life. We get hold of the wrong story about who did what, or we blame individuals and groups for a large systemic problem that they didn't cause. We overestimate trivial wrongs and also, sometimes, underestimate important ones. We obsess about our own relative status (or that of our group). We think that payback will solve the problems created by the original offense, even though it does not.

But there is more. We impute blame, often, even when there is no blame to be apportioned. The world is full of accidents. Sometimes a disaster is just a disaster. Sometimes illness and hardship are just illness and hardship. The medical profession can't keep us completely safe from disease and death, and the wisest and most just social policies will not prevent economic woes arising from natural disasters or badly understood economic trends. But in our monarchical way we expect the world to be made for our service. It gratifies our ego, and is in a deep sense comforting, to think that any bad event is someone's fault. The act of pinning blame and pursuing the "bad guy" is deeply consoling. It makes us feel control rather than helplessness.

Psychologists have done a lot of research on people's instinctual views of the way the world works, and they find that people have a deep-rooted need to believe that the world is just. One aspect of this "just world hypothesis" is the tendency to believe that people who are badly off cause their own misery by laziness or bad conduct.[14] But another related aspect of this "just world" belief is the need to believe that when we encounter loss and

[14]There is by now a large literature on these phenomena. A good starting point is Melvin J. Lerner, *The Belief in a Just World: A Fundamental Delusion* (New York: Springer, 1980). An important article relating the phenomenon to New Deal efforts to shift the perception that the US poor are shiftless and lazy is Richard J. McAdams, "*The Grapes of Wrath* and the Role of Luck in Economic Outcomes," in Alison LaCroix, Saul Levmore, and Martha C. Nussbaum, eds., *Power, Prose, Purse: Law, Literature, and Economic Transformations* (New York: Oxford University Press, 2018).

adversity it isn't just loss, it is someone's wrongdoing, and that we can somehow recoup our loss by punishing the "bad guy."

Your parent dies in the hospital. It is very human to believe that "the doctors did it," and to deflect one's grief into malpractice litigation. Your marriage falls apart. Often there is fault somewhere, but sometimes it can't be easily identified. Things do just fall apart. Still, it is human to fix blame on the "bad" spouse and try to crush that person with litigation. It makes life look more intelligible, the universe more just.

Economic woes are sometimes caused by an identifiable person or persons' malfeasance, and sometimes by clearly stupid or unfair policies; but more often their cause is obscure and uncertain. We feel bad saying that: it makes the world look messy and ungovernable. So why not pin the blame—as the Greeks did—on groups that are easy to demonize: in place of their rhetorical category of "barbarians" we might focus blame on immigrants, or women entering the workforce, or bankers, or rich people. The Salem witch trials were once thought to be the result of group hysteria among adolescent girls. But now we know that a preponderant number of the witch blamers were young men entering adulthood, afflicted by the usual woes of an insecure colony in a new world: economic uncertainty, a harsh climate, political instability. How easy, then, to blame the whole thing on witches, usually elderly unpopular women, who can easily be targeted and whose death brings a temporary satisfaction to the mind.

Our earliest fairy tales have this structure. Hansel and Gretel wander into the woods to search for food. The problem is hunger, compounded by the fact that their parents have to work at menial jobs and have no leisure to care for the children. But the story tells us that these very real problems are unreal, and that the real problem is a witch who lives in the woods, and turns little children into gingerbread. Red Riding Hood goes to visit her grandmother, walking a long distance alone. The real problem in this story is aging and lack of care: the family lives far away, and Grandmother is not doing well. But quickly the story deflects our attention: the problem is not this difficult human problem at all, requiring a structural solution: it is a single wolf who has broken into Grandmother's house. In both stories, when the ugly villain is killed, the world is just fine. Our love of an orderly universe makes these simple fictional solutions tempting. It's hard to wrap our minds around complicated truths, and it's far easier to incinerate the witch than to live with hope in a world that is not made for human delectation.

ANGER, CHILD OF FEAR

Anger is a distinct emotion with distinctive thoughts. It looks manly and important, not at all timorous. Nonetheless, it is the offspring of fear.[15] How so?

First, if we were not plagued by great vulnerability, we would probably never get angry. Lucretius imagined the gods as beings who are perfect and complete, beyond our world, and he said, "They are not enslaved by gratitude, nor are they

[15]To me, the failure to give explicit recognition to this link is a serious flaw in recent sociological analyses of American anger: see, for example, Arlie Russell Hochschild, *Strangers in Their Own Land: Anger and Mourning on the American Right* (New York: The New Press, 2016).

tainted by anger."[16] If anger is a response to a significant damage inflicted by someone else on you or someone or something you care about, then a person who is complete, who cannot be damaged, has no room for anger. (Judeo-Christian pictures of divine anger imagine God as loving humans and as deeply vulnerable to their misdeeds.)

Some moral reformers have urged us to become like Lucretius's gods. The Greek Stoics thought that we should learn not to care at all about the "goods of fortune," that is, anything that can be damaged by anything outside our own control. Then we would lose fear, and in the bargain, we'd lose anger. Philosophy Richard Sorabji has shown that Gandhi's views were very close to those of the Stoics.[17]

The problem, however, is that in losing fear we also lose love. The basis of both is a strong attachment to someone or something outside our control. There is nothing that makes us more vulnerable than loving other people, or loving a country. So much can go wrong. Fear is often rational, and grief an omnipresent reality. In one half year the Roman philosopher and politician Cicero lost the two things he loved most in the world, when his daughter Tullia died in childbirth and the Roman Republic collapsed into tyranny. Even though his friends thought his grief excessive and urged him to be a proper Stoic, he told his best friend Atticus that he could not

[16]This passage occurs in book I, lines 44–49 and also in book II; it probably belongs in both places, though the first is often bracketed. It is such an important point that Lucretius wants to emphasize it.

[17]Richard Sorabji, *Gandhi and the Stoics: Modern Experiments in Ancient Values* (Chicago: University of Chicago Press, 2012).

stop grieving, and, what's more, he didn't think he ought to.[18] Taking the measure of love fully means suffering. So, the solution that wipes out both fear and anger with one stroke is not one we should accept. Keeping love means keeping a lot of fear.

And though that does not necessarily mean keeping retributive anger, it makes it a lot harder to win the struggle with anger. Fear is not only a necessary precondition for anger, it is also a poison to anger, feeding the four errors. When we are afraid, we jump to conclusions, lashing out before we have thought carefully about the who and the how. When problems are complex and their causes poorly understood, as economic problems tend to be, fear often leads us to pin blame on individuals or groups and then to conduct witch-hunts, rather than pausing to figure things out.

Fear also feeds obsession with relative status: when people feel bigger than others, they think they can't be destroyed. But when people protect their vulnerable egos by thoughts of status, they can easily be goaded into anger, since the world is full of insults and slights. Indeed, Lucretius traces all status competition to fear, arguing that it is a way of soothing ourselves: by putting others down we make ourselves feel powerful.[19]

And fear also feeds the focus on payback, since vulnerable people think that getting back at wrongdoers, even obliterating them, is a way of reestablishing lost control and dignity.

[18]The *Letters to Atticus* are superbly edited and translated in four volumes in the Loeb Classical Library, by David Shackleton Bailey. I discuss the Tullia letters in Martha C. Nussbaum and Saul Levmore, *Aging Thoughtfully* (New York: Oxford University Press, 2017).

[19]Book III.59–64, 74-8, see further discussion in chapter 5.

Lucretius even traces war to fear: feeling insecure, we rage against what threatens us and seek to obliterate it. He omits the obvious possibility that war may be caused by a reasonable reaction to a genuine threat to our safety and our values, and thus to a fear that is rational.[20] So we should not accept his analysis fully. I am no pacifist, nor were my primary heroes of non-anger, Martin Luther King Jr. and Nelson Mandela. Gandhi, I think, made a large mistake by endorsing total pacifism. But even just wars, such as I believe the Second World War to have been, are often marred by zeal for the blood of the aggressor, and one could certainly argue that episodes such as the bombing of Dresden were motivated by payback rather than sound policy. Great leaders understand that we need to retain and fortify the spirit of determined protest against wrongdoing, without comforting ourselves with retributive thinking. The brilliant speech in which Winston Churchill said, "I have nothing to offer but blood, toil, tears, and sweat," refers to danger, to struggle, and to a willingness to accept great pain in order to preserve democratic values. It is conspicuous for its utter lack of retributivism. Churchill does *not* say that paying back the Nazis will remove the threat to freedom. Freedom is beautiful, and we must be prepared to suffer for it, but we must focus on defending what we love rather than "disgorging [our] venom on the land," as Aeschylus's Furies put it. Churchill's

[20]See book III.73. He blames fear for civil war only, a leading problem in Rome in his day. He does not comment on foreign wars, and leaves open the possibility that these are reasonable—since he is aiming to persuade his interlocutor Memmius, a Roman in the military who has taken a brief pause within the fighting.

speech is of a piece with the best Allied aims to rebuild Germany postwar, and we can now see the wisdom of that course, as Germany is among our most valuable allies.

Finally, helplessness, and the fear that goes with it, lead to the reflex in which we pin blame on someone in order to feel less buffeted by fortune and more in control. Even a long and difficult fight (a protracted malpractice lawsuit, divorce litigation lasting many years) is often psychologically preferable to accepting loss.

PROTEST WITHOUT PAYBACK

What's the alternative? We can keep the spirit of determined protest against injustice while letting go of the empty fantasy of payback. This forward-looking strategy includes protesting wrongdoing when it occurs, but not imputing wrongdoing where there is, instead, the murky thicket of the global economy to manage, outsourcing, and automation to reconcile with our citizens' welfare. Never seizing hold of blame as a substitute for a feeling of powerlessness but also not yielding to despair. Even when we are confident in imputing wrongdoing to an individual or a group, we can still firmly refuse payback, but look to the future with hope, choosing strategies designed to make things better rather than to inflict the maximum pain.

Let's consider just one example of protest without payback: the ideas of Martin Luther King Jr., who contributed so much to our society's ongoing struggle with racism and its search for justice. King always said that anger had a limited usefulness, in that it brought people to his protest movement, rather than sitting in despair. But once they got there, the anger had to be "purified" and "channelized."[21] What he means is that people must give up the payback wish and yet keep the spirit of justified protest. Instead of retribution, they need hope, and faith in the possibility of justice. In an essay of 1959, he says that the struggle for integration will continue to encounter obstacles, and that these obstacles can be met in two very different ways:

> One is the development of a wholesome social organization to resist with effective, firm measures any efforts to impede progress. The other is a confused, anger-motivated drive to strike back violently, to inflict damage. Primarily, it seeks to cause injury to retaliate for wrongful suffering . . . It is punitive—not radical or constructive.[22]

King, of course, was characterizing not just a deep-seated human tendency, but the actual ideas and sentiments of Malcolm X, as he understood them.[23]

King insisted constantly that his approach did not mean acquiescence in injustice: there is still an urgent demand, there is

[21]I analyze most of the relevant texts within King's writings in "From Anger to Love: Self-Purification and Political Resistance," in Tommie Shelby, ed., *To Shape a New World: Essays on the Political Philosophy of Martin Luther King, Jr.* (Cambridge, MA: Harvard University Press, 2018). Some passages references are also given in *Anger and Forgiveness*, ch. 7.

[22]James M. Washington, ed., *A Testament of Hope: The Essential Writings and Speeches of Martin Luther King, Jr.* (New York: HarperCollins, 1986), 32.

[23]Those ideas are also discussed in "From Anger to Love." And see especially Malcolm's "Message to the Grassroots," in George Breitman, ed., *Malcolm X Speaks* (New York: Grove Press, 1965).

still a protest against unjust conditions, in which the protester takes great risks with his or her body, in what King called "direct action." Still, the protester's focus must turn to the future that all must work to create together, with hope and faith in the possibility of justice.

King, in short, favors and exemplifies what I've called Transition-Anger: the protest part of anger without the payback. To see this better, let's study the sequence of emotions in his "I Have a Dream" speech.[24] King begins, indeed, with what looks like a summons to anger: he points to the wrongful injuries of racism, which have failed to fulfill the nation's implicit promises of equality. One hundred years after the Emancipation Proclamation, "the life of the Negro is still sadly crippled by the manacles of segregation and the chains of discrimination."

The next move King makes is significant: for instead of demonizing white Americans, he calmly compares them to people who have defaulted on a financial obligation: "America has given the Negro people a bad check, a check which has come back marked 'insufficient funds.' " This begins the shift to what I've called Transition-Anger: for it makes us think ahead in non-retributive ways. The essential question is not how whites can be humiliated, but how can this debt be paid, and in the financial metaphor, the thought of destroying the debtor is not likely to be central.

The future now takes over, as King focuses on a time in

[24]I analyze the speech in *Anger and Forgiveness*, ch. 2, but this is a new analysis with nuances of difference. The speech itself is widely available online.

which all may join together in pursuing justice and honoring obligations: "But we refuse to believe that the bank of justice is bankrupt. We refuse to believe that there are insufficient funds in the great vaults of opportunity of this nation." No mention, again, of torment or payback, only of determination to ensure the protection of civil rights at last. King reminds his audience that the moment is urgent, and that there is a danger of rage spilling over: but he repudiates that behavior in advance. "In the process of gaining our rightful place, we must not be guilty of wrongful deeds. Let us not seek to satisfy our thirst for freedom by drinking from the cup of bitterness and hatred . . . Again and again, we must rise to the majestic heights of meeting physical force with soul force."

So, the "payback" is reconceived as the vindication of civil rights, a process that unites black and white in a quest for freedom and justice. Everyone benefits: as many white people already recognize, "their freedom is inextricably bound to our freedom."

King next repudiates a despair that could lead to the abandonment of effort. It is at this point that the most famous section of the speech, "I Have a Dream," takes flight. And of course, this dream is one not of retributive punishment but of equality, liberty, and brotherhood. In pointed terms, King invites the African American members of his audience to imagine brotherhood even with their former tormentors:

> I have a dream that one day on the red hills of Georgia, the sons of former slaves and the sons of former slave owners will be able to sit down together at the table of brotherhood.

> I have a dream that one day even the state of Mississippi, a state sweltering with the heat of injustice, sweltering with the heat of oppression, will be transformed into an oasis of freedom and justice . . .
>
> I have a dream that one day, down in Alabama, with its vicious racists, with its governor having his lips dripping with the words "interposition" and "nullification"—one day right there in Alabama little black boys and black girls will be able to join hands with little white boys and white girls as sisters and brothers.

There is indeed outrage in this speech, and the outrage summons up a vision of rectification, which might easily take a retributive form. But King gets busy right away reshaping retributivism into work and hope. For how, sanely and really, could injustice be made good by retributive payback? The oppressor's pain and lowering do not make the afflicted free. Only an intelligent and imaginative effort toward justice can do that.

It might seem strange to compare King to Aeschylus, though it's really not strange at all, given King's vast learning in literature and philosophy. He's basically saying the same thing: democracy must give up the empty and destructive thought of payback and move toward a future of legal justice and human well-being. King's opponents portrayed his stance as weak. Malcolm X said sardonically that it was like coffee that has had so much milk poured into it that it has turned white and cold, and doesn't even taste like coffee.[25] But that was wrong. King's stance is strong, not weak. He resists one of the most powerful of human impulses, the retributive impulse, for the sake of the future. One of the trickiest problems in politics is to persist in a determined search for solutions, without letting fear deflect us onto the track of anger's errors. The idea that Aeschylus and King share is that democratic citizens should face with courage the problems and, yes, the outrageous injustices, that we encounter in political and social life. Lashing out in anger and fear does not solve these problems; instead, it leads, as it did in both Athens and Rome, to a spiral of retributive violence.

Lucretius tells a grim tale of human anger and fear gone wild. He imagines a world not unlike his own, in which insecurity leads to acts of aggression, which do not quiet insecurity. (At the time when he wrote, the Roman Republic was imploding, and insecurity, mounting everywhere, would shortly give way to tyranny.) In an effort to quiet fear, he imagines, people get more and more aggressive—until they think up a new way to inflict maximum damage on their enemies: putting wild beasts to work in the military.[26]

> They even tried out bulls in the service of war.
> They practiced letting wild boars loose against their enemies.
> They even used fierce lions as an advance guard, equipped

[25]See "Message to the Grassroots," in George Breitman, ed., *Malcolm X Speaks* (New York: Grove Press, 1965).
[26]Lucretius V.1308–49, my translation.

With a special force of armed and ferocious trainers
To hold them in check and keep them in harness.
It was no use.
The lions, hot with blood, broke ranks wildly.
Trampled the troops, tossing their manes.

In a poetic tour de force, Lucretius now imagines the carnage the animals unleash. Then he pulls back. Did this really happen?, he says. Maybe it happened in some other world out in space. And what, he says, did those fictional people want to accomplish? To inflict great pain on the enemy—even if it meant that they would perish themselves!

Lucretius's point is that our retributive emotions are those wild beasts. People may think anger powerful, but it always gets out of hand and turns back on us. And, yet worse, half the time people don't care. They're so deeply sunk in payback fantasies that they'd prefer to accomplish nothing, so long as they *make those people suffer*. His grim science-fiction fantasy reminds us that we'll always defeat ourselves so long as we let ourselves be governed by fear, anger, and the politics of blame.

There is a better alternative. Aeschylus knew it, and King both knew and lived it. Making a future of justice and well-being is hard. It requires self-examination, personal risk, searching critical arguments, and uncertain initiatives to make common cause with opponents—in a spirit of hope and what we could call rational faith.

One crucial part of this forward movement is to follow King in separating the doer from the deed, embracing the humanity in others while protesting the wrongs they may have committed. In that way, we can begin to think of our fellow citizens as our friends, even if we don't approve of what they are saying and doing. But in the fear-blame-payback mode we don't see any good in others. And it's all too easy, especially these days in our social media world, to form not constructive networks but networks of blame. When we think this way, we invite the wild beasts to help us, and it's no wonder if they then take over and dig in their claws.

4

FEAR-DRIVEN DISGUST: THE POLITICS OF EXCLUSION

All societies marginalize or subordinate some groups of people. In feudal societies and monarchies, subordination is part of the official theory of governance: nobles are better than peasants and should dominate them, the king has a divine right to lord it over others. In modern democracies, by contrast, the public norm is usually one of equal respect and equal consideration. So, group subordination, when it occurs, violates the society's own norms of justice. We know, however, that democratic citizens are not a breed apart, but simply human, prone to all the failings to which fear and self-defensiveness lead the best of us, unless those tendencies are held firmly in check. We'd predict, then, that democratic citizens would need both good social norms and good laws to shore up equal respect—and that even when those are present, defection would all too easily take place in times of stress or uncertainty.

Our society (like most) has an ugly history of exclusion based on race, gender, sexual orientation, disability, age, and religion. In our current political moment, demands for equality and dignity by previously excluded groups are met, distressingly often, by hate propaganda and even hate crimes. We actually know all too little about the number of hate groups and hate crimes. According to the Southern Poverty Law Center, which has compiled data on hate crimes for years, the number of hate groups has risen from 892 in 2015 to 917 in 2016.[1] According to the Center for the Study of Hate and Extremism at California State University, San Bernardino, hate crimes in nine metropolitan areas in the US increased by over 20 percent last year.[2] And according to a 2015 FBI report that breaks down hate crimes by type, 59.2 percent were motivated by racial bias, 19.7 percent by religious bias (of which the largest number were anti-Jewish, but an increasing number were anti-Muslim), and 17.7 percent by sexual orientation bias.[3]

Data are not reliable in this area. As then-director of the FBI James Comey stated in 2014, "We need to do a better job of tracking and reporting hate crime to fully understand what is

[1]https://www.splcenter.org/news/2017/02/15/hate-groups-increase-second-consecutive-year-trump-electrifies-radical-right.

[2]https://csbs.csusb.edu/hate-and-extremism-center. This site contains all the reports produced by the center.

[3]https://www.fbi.gov/news/stories/2015-hate-crime-statistics-released, https://www.fbi.gov/news/pressrel/press-releases/fbi-releases-2015-hate-crime-statistics.

happening in our communities and how to stop it."[4] Part of the apparent increase in such crimes is surely the result of better data gathering and more reporting. So, we should not panic or immediately blame Trump supporters for an alleged upsurge. Instead, remembering that the United States has an ugly history of hate crimes and animus, especially in the area of race, but including, as well, crimes motivated by religion, gender, and sexual orientation, we should simply say that whether there is an increase or not, there is too much hate crime and we should figure out how to stop it. The ugly resurgence of white supremacism and anti-Semitism in the August 2017 march in Charlottesville, Virginia, has brought this long-simmering issue into the open.

One factor my philosophical analysis will not consider is the easy availability of guns in the United States. All countries have hatred and hate crimes, but what might be a beating in Europe all too often becomes a multi-victim gun attack in our country. I believe that this is a huge part of the current problem of hate crime, but that's not my topic. Fortunately (since it is politically impossible to make progress on this issue today), there are other things to discuss!

Finding remedies means understanding the roots of these problems. A philosophical-psychological analysis of the emotions of exclusion will clarify where we are, and where we might go, how we might pursue greater reciprocity and equality.

[4]Comey's remarks, made in a speech to the Anti-Defamation League in 2014, are cited in the FBI's 2015 report, at https://www.fbi.gov/news/stories/2015-hate-crime-statistics-released, repeated the call for more data in 2017, see http://www.jta.org/2017/05/09/news-opinion/politics/fbi-director-james-comey-calls-for-better-ways-to-track-hate-crimes.

How does exclusion work? What emotions drive and shape it? And what role does fear play in the creation of such hierarchies? Fear drives a lot of bad behavior in this area, especially when fear is combined with the anger-blame dynamic. Fear and related anger are especially salient in hate crimes against Muslims, where a tidal wave of fear can be easily deflected onto the track of blame and retributive violence. At this point, however, there is another emotion that we need to consider. Like anger, this emotion is infected by fear, and fear often leads this emotion, and thereby us, astray. Unlike anger, however, this emotion does not require wrongdoing or the threat of wrongdoing to get going. It is motivated by anxiety about animality and mortality, and triggered, therefore, by bodily characteristics, real or imputed, that bear a close relationship to our anxieties about mortality and the vulnerable animal body.

That emotion is disgust. The irrationalities of this emotion underlie many social evils.[5]

Let's return to fairy tales. Witches and ogres are not just

[5]I have written about disgust in two earlier books: *Hiding from Humanity: Disgust, Shame, and the Law* (Princeton: Princeton University Press, 2004), and *From Disgust to Humanity: Sexual Orientation and Constitutional Law* (New York: Oxford University Press, 2010); the former studies the emotions of disgust and shame from a psychological and philosophical perspective and then considers examples from a wide range of types of prejudice; the latter focuses on sexual orientation and the role of disgust in prejudice in that area. More recently, I've organized a two-country comparative study of disgust and stigma with colleagues in India, issuing in the volume *The Empire of Disgust: Prejudice, Discrimination, and Policy in India and the US*, edited by Zoya Hasan, Aziz Huq, Martha C. Nussbaum, and Vidhu Verma, forthcoming with Oxford University Press, Delhi. The volume considers disgust in relation to prejudice along lines of caste, race, gender, sexual

threatening, they are also ugly and deformed. Often, they are ugly in a particular way: they disgust us. Their bodies are imagined as unclean, or slimy, or smelly, and often they even take the form of animals who have those characteristics (frogs, snakes, bats). Shakespeare knew what he was doing when he depicted the witches in *Macbeth* as associates of such foul animals: into their brew go "fillet of a fenny snake," "eye of newt and toe of frog," and so forth.

And Shakespeare also knew how readily sliminess and grossness get projected onto to the bodies of human minorities who are viewed as undesirable: the witches also add to their broth a "liver of blaspheming Jew," as well as a "Nose of Turk and Tartar's lips," and "finger of birth-strangl'd babe / Ditch-deliver'd by a drab." Ethnic and sexual minorities (Jews, Muslims, prostitutes) are listed alongside disgusting slimy animals as if their bodies were themselves slimy and disgusting. That dead baby's finger was delivered in a sewer by a female prostitute, and thus tainted by the filth of feces, urine, and sexual fluids.

But we are anticipating. I'll return later to these choice examples of "projective disgust." First, then, "primary disgust."

PRIMARY DISGUST AND VULNERABILITY

Disgust would seem to be an especially visceral emotion. Its common reflex is to vomit or at least to say "Yuck." And disgust,

---

orientation, disability, age, class, and Muslim identity. (There are two essays on each topic, permitting divergent perspectives and arguments.)

like fear, is likely to be part of our evolutionary heritage. Unlike fear, however, it is not present in very young children, who love to play with their own feces until they are taught otherwise. In fact, disgust is first observed at the time of toilet training. This does not mean that it is totally a learned behavior. A tendency may be innate and yet take time to develop, as happens with language. It does mean, however, that culture has a lot of time to shape it, and that we should be alert for those culturally specific formations.

I'll use the term "primary disgust" to refer to a "yuck" reaction to bodily excrements and other bodily fluids (blood, snot, semen, ear wax, vomit, and urine are all typically found disgusting), and also to animals who seem to share with those substances sensory properties such as foulness, sliminess, smelliness—all the things the witches put into their cauldron. Shakespeare also includes toads, lizards, and bats; to our own cauldron we would surely add cockroaches, houseflies, bedbugs, probably rats. German has a generic term for these: *Ungeziefer*. That is what Gregor Samsa, in Kafka's *Metamorphosis* finds himself turned into, and Kafka's intention, which no translation can capture, is to leave the species of disgusting creature unclear. It is sort of like a cockroach, but it is much larger and has long legs. The main distinguishing feature of the Gregor-*Ungeziefer* is the disgust its presence elicits.

To the list of disgust elicitors we must add, as well, and importantly: animal and human corpses. Indeed, perhaps this aversion is key to all the others, in that the idea of decay seems to run like a connecting thread through all the other objects of primary disgust.

We might initially think that primary disgust is a simple non-cognitive sensory reaction. However, an important body of psychological research by Paul Rozin and his colleagues has shown that this is not the case: disgust has a marked cognitive content.[6] On the one hand, experiments show that disgust is not the same thing as a simple sensory reaction. The very same smell elicits different reactions depending on what the subject thinks it is coming from. Subjects sniff a vial containing an unknown substance. People who think the smell comes from cheese usually like it; people who are told it comes from feces usually find it disgusting. (The real smells are very similar.) When you think it is cheese, you probably also think it is a nice thing to put into your mouth. When you are disgusted, thinking it is feces, your disgust propels you away, and you would never put it into your mouth. Disgust, researchers conclude, involves the thought that the object is a contaminant: something bad to ingest, or even perhaps to touch. The mouth is an especially charged boundary.

We all avoid eating things that are dangerous, and feces are in fact dangerous to eat, as are corpses and many of those slimy animals. So, the next hypothesis researchers tested is that disgust is a type of fear of the dangerous. There is some truth to this hypothesis, in the sense that there is a certain rough correlation between the disgusting and the dangerous, and disgust may well have evolved as a mechanism protecting us from dangers coming from decay and bacteria. It has a limited

[6]I discuss Rozin's research (and that of his colleagues) in detail with comprehensive citations in *Hiding from Humanity*.

usefulness as a heuristic even when we know a lot about danger. Thus, it's a good idea to throw out milk that smells disgusting rather than to spend time testing it for bacteria.

Still, research shows that disgust is different from a fear reaction to danger. Many dangerous things are not disgusting: poisonous mushrooms are an obvious example. And many things are found disgusting even when there is no danger at all, or the danger has been removed. Urine, semen, and blood are not dangerous to ingest, and sweat is just a form of urine, dangerous only if there are also bacteria in the vicinity. (Put differently, it's not the sweat that's dangerous, it's the skin of the sweaty person.) So, our refusal to ingest such things has to have a different explanation. Why are they grouped with feces and snot, which really are dangerous? Furthermore, experimental subjects refuse to ingest sterilized cockroaches or to drink juice stirred with a sterilized flyswatter. One experiment involved sealing a sterilized cockroach inside an indigestible plastic capsule that would come out unaltered in the subject's feces. People still refused to swallow it. So perceived danger does not really explain people's aversion to ingesting certain sorts of things.

Things become even more complicated when we recognize that disgust uses a symbolic vocabulary of shape and contact. (Rozin calls this "magical thinking.") Thus, people refuse to eat fudge shaped like dog feces, even when they know what it is. They also refuse to drink juice out of a sterilized vessel shaped like a bedpan. And contact matters: if something has touched the disgusting, it becomes disgusting, however much we clean it. Thus, if a rat has eaten off a plate, people don't want to use that plate again, no matter how often it has been washed.

Disgust, researchers conclude, is an aversion to contact that is motivated by a thought of contamination. This thought may involve danger, but it may also simply involve a refusal to *be* that thing, to have that (base) thing inside you as a part of you. The idea that "you are what you eat" has been cited by researchers as the folk belief underlying this way of thinking. There is a kind of anxiety underlying disgust, clearly, since its bodily reflex is aversion and often flight. But the anxiety isn't simple fear of danger, given its symbolic nature. Rozin notices that all the objects of (primary) disgust are animals or animal substances (with the possible exception of some slimy plants such as okra, which some people find disgusting). And he concludes that the objects of disgust are "animal reminders," things that make us think of our own animality and, hence, mortality.

Rozin moves too quickly here, as I argued in 2004, and as some subsequent researchers emphasize. We do not feel disgusted by all aspects of our animality, such as strength and speed; nor are we revolted by animals who embody those characteristics. We are disgusted by what we think of as base or debasing, including prominently that which either is dead and decaying or which reminds us of the stench of death and decay. So, we should not be too hasty in separating disgust from fear and from the avoidance of harmful pathogens. Disgust is infused by some type of fear, but—and here Rozin is correct—it is a fear that lies deeper than the mere thought that this or that thing is dangerous. It is a fear that somehow pertains to death and our potentially decaying embodiment, and that is what makes it operate through symbols, rather than simply through sensory properties. We are quite literally refusing to ingest decay, hence to be "dead."

Human beings in all cultures, and alone among the animals, exhibit anxiety about being animals. We seek to conceal the signs of our animality and shrink from them when they are thrust upon us. Jonathan Swift's poem "The Lady's Dressing-Room"[7] is a marvelous depiction of this universal human tendency. The woman spends five hours washing and dressing, creating a pretense that she is a "Goddess," "sweet and cleanly," "array'd in Lace, Brocades, and Tissues." But her lover sneaks into her dressing room and finds all the signs of her animality: snot, ear wax, dandruff, hairs plucked from her chin, clothes with sweaty armpits, skin oil, a basin with "the scrapings of her Teeth and Gums," stockings that smell like "stinking toes"—all of which "turn'd poor Strephon's Bowels." The climax of his revulsion arrives when he opens the laundry chest, a veritable Pandora's box of evils—and finds evidence of urine and feces (perhaps also menstrual fluids, "Things, which must not be exprest").

"Thus finishing his grand Survey, / Disgusted Strephon stole away / Repeating in his amorous Fits, / Oh! Celia, Celia, Celia shits!" If Swift is unusually obsessive about such matters, he gives voice to a profound human anxiety, and he is correct that much of human life (certainly not just female life) is taken

[7]For the full text, see https://www.poetryfoundation.org/poems/50579/the-ladys-dressing-room.

up by routines through which we try not to disgust others, or ourselves.

Nor should we think that these anxieties are from a long-gone era. The need for a goddess-like Celia is omnipresent on Internet porn sites, which strip women of pubic hair, wrinkles, secretions, menstrual and other, and of course subtract all smell. Women then are expected to make themselves into that type of airbrushed Celia; to the extent that they don't succeed, they are at risk of being found disgusting.

What is all this about? The name "Goddess" tells us: it's about transcending our mortal bodily humanity, concealing death and decay from both self and others. No other animal does exactly that. And women have often been expected to do that especially obsessively. All animals fear death in a straightforward way, shrinking from pain and the ending of a life. Many animal species bury feces, and many also abandon aging or disabled members. But we are the only animals who turn our aversion to death into a strange symbolic project of transcendence, what the great primate researcher Frans de Waal calls "anthropodenial," denial of our membership in that animal species.

Even primary disgust, reasonably useful when confined to bodily fluids and smelly and sticky objects, is, then, infused with fear. It expresses what anthropologist Ernest Becker called the "denial of death," and it is not just denial, it is flight.[8] Even though I've called this "primary" and suggested that it is relatively unshaped by cultural differences, it certainly has a

[8]See Ernest Becker, *The Denial of Death* (New York: Free Press, 1973).

complicated symbolic content, expressing a doomed and yet all-important human project.

PROJECTIVE DISGUST AND GROUP SUBORDINATION

Disgust, as we saw, begins to appear during toilet training. Culture thus has a chance to shape it. Individuals and cultures vary to some extent in the messages they transmit about bodily humanity, how good or how awful it is. But there is no known society, and possibly no individual, who fully and consistently exemplifies Walt Whitman's ideal, embracing the "body electric" with love and without shrinking.[9] Maybe we shouldn't even want that, since the human struggle to transcend mortality probably lies at the root of many scientific and cultural advances.

Disgust, however, does not stop with those "primary objects," bodily fluids, animals with similar properties, and corpses. Disgust ramifies outward, and its cultural form becomes, as time goes on, more and more complex. The flight from animality and death takes a highly problematic form: it becomes what I shall call *projective disgust*.

The project of defining our "higher" status against the "mere" animal is insecure. Because we are always deceiving ourselves when we think of ourselves as above the animal, our stratagems are flimsy and easily unmasked. Every day in countless ways our animal bodies compel our attention. Right

[9]"I Sing the Body Electric" is part of Whitman's *Leaves of Grass*.

now, as I write this sentence, I have to pee, and I am trying to decide how long I can continue working before I just have to take a bathroom break. Even if we turn in aversion from the objects of primary disgust, trying to keep ourselves pure from all contamination, we don't succeed very well. However much we wash and brush and floss and wipe and open the window, we still make almost constant contact with our own secretions and those of others. Some aversion to bodily secretions is rationally motivated by fear of danger. Thus, like most singers, I am pretty phobic about sneezers and coughers. But a lot of it is true disgust, and it is difficult to keep the disgusting at bay.

We keep ourselves at bay successfully, indeed, only in high literature, where the bodily functions are usually never mentioned. Swift is shocking, even in the more receptive domain of satire and the comic. But what is oddly called the "realist novel" is an instructive case of how avoidance became normative for an entire genre. Lots of reality is indeed in the "realist novel," lots of details of people and places, even food. The physicality of nature is powerfully present, even when dangerous. But the whole terrain of the disgusting (until relatively recently) has been banished. No toilets, no toothbrushing, no menstrual periods, no drippy noses, no sexual fluids. Dead people but no corpses, meaning no references to stench and decay. When James Joyce suddenly showed Leopold Bloom going to the outhouse, and, later, masturbating while looking up Gerty MacDowell's skirt, and when he represented Molly Bloom ruminating about the penises of her lovers while going to the chamber pot, as her menstrual period arrives, the public was shocked. "All the secret sewers of vice are canalized in its flow of unimaginable thoughts, images, and pornographic words," wrote an early reviewer.[10] So great was readers' horror of looking at themselves that the representation of the daily seemed like monstrous vice. When D. H. Lawrence represented sexual intercourse explicitly, he too was charged with being foul and "obscene," a word that has its derivation from the Latin word *caenum*, or filth. Indeed, the very legal definition of the obscene, judges have noted, makes reference to the disgusting.[11]

So, people keep running up against themselves, however hard they try not to. However: if people can't keep entirely clear of the disgusting in themselves, they may be helped by a further stratagem that is all too common in human life. Here's the "bright idea": what if we could identify a group of human beings whom we could see as more animal than we are, more sweaty, more smelly, more sexual, more suffused with the stench of mortality? If we could identify such a group of humans and subordinate them successfully, we might feel more secure. *Those* are the animals, not us. *Those* are dirty and smelly, *we* are pure and clean. And they are beneath us; we dominate them. This type of confused thinking is ubiquitous in human societies as a way of creating distance between ourselves and our problematic animality.

Think of fairy tales again. Young children all too often learn

[10]James Douglas, in the *Sunday Express*, 1922, Quoted in David Bradshaw, "James Douglas: The Sanitary Inspector of Literature," in *Prudes on the Prowl: Fiction and Obscenity in England, 1850 to the Present Day*, ed. by David Bradshaw and Rachel Potter (Oxford: Oxford University Press, 2013), 90–110 (97–98).

[11]See *Hiding from Humanity*, ch. 3, for the history of relevant obscenity law.

to calm their fears not through rational thought about how to protect themselves from hunger, disease, and the other dangers of life. Instead, all too often, they are encouraged by the stories they hear to pin blame onto an ugly, deformed, bestial figure, an ogre or a witch, or even a talking animal, and they tell themselves that if they can control and dominate those figures, projections of what they fear in themselves, life will be more secure. As far back as ancient Rome, witches have been depicted as disgusting and foul.[12]

In fairy tales the villain is usually an individual, but in social life the disgusting is often projected outward on to a vulnerable group. The witches in *Macbeth* toss into their cauldron the Jew, the Turk or Muslim, symbolized by his nose, and the Tartar, probably a black African (Tartarus is a mythological region of blackness), symbolized by his lips. If we can avoid contamination from those people, we can somehow avoid, and rise above, our own animality.

That's the idea behind what I call *projective disgust*. It seems like a crazy, doomed project. Humanity is pretty much the same everywhere, so how could such segmentations be made? And won't they be sure to collapse of themselves, as the subordinated group attests its own similar humanity? Projective disgust is called "projective" because it sends disgust-properties

[12]See Debbie Felton, "Witches, Disgust, and Anti-abortion Propaganda in Imperial Rome," in Donald Lateiner and Dimos Spatharas, *The Ancient Emotion of Disgust* (New York: Oxford University Press, 2017), 189–201; Felton argues that the emphasis on disgusting witches in this period was connected to underlying anxiety about women's sexual freedom, including the practice of abortion.

away from the self and on to other people, saying "They are smelly and bestial." But won't that focus on imputing disgust-properties to others be sure to turn "our" (the dominant group's) gaze back on ourselves, making "us" aware that what "we" target and flee in others is our very own selves?

Nonetheless, projective disgust is prominent in every known society. Some groups targeted for disgust-subordination are racial subgroups, identified by their skin color or other surface features. And we know how a bogus race science was created to sustain the lie that those groups (African Americans, Asians, Native Americans) are really "other," a different species from "us." Other groups are targeted on the basis of a religious-ethnic group membership: Jews, Muslims. Other groups are targeted because their non-mainstream sexuality draws attention to itself. In many societies gays, lesbians, and transgender people are found disgusting because their bodily and sexual nature stands out, compels fascination: they seem more bodily somehow. Campaigns against equal rights for gays in the US used images of anal intercourse and the alleged mixing of feces and blood to encourage the public to shrink from social contact with gay people, and gay men especially, in housing and employment.[13]

Still other groups are found disgusting because they straightforwardly remind the dominant group of their own weakness, their own future. Thus, the former "untouchables" in the Indian caste hierarchy were those who disposed of feces

[13]In *From Disgust to Humanity*, I give examples of the pamphlet literature circulated in the campaign against non-discrimination laws in Colorado.

and corpses and who swept the floors. By avoiding bodily contact with them, people somehow fantasized that they avoided contact with the "dirt" in themselves—despite the fact that every day they themselves excreted the wastes the lower castes were carrying, and despite the fact that they saw humans dying in all social groups. Thus, too, in every society people with severe mental and physical disabilities have been shunned as revolting, as if avoiding those instances of disability made people invulnerable to disabilities of their own. A special revulsion often greets the aging body, since that is the one group that everyone knows they will end up in sooner or later, unless they die prematurely. Keeping one's distance from wrinkled and halting bodies makes people feel better, as if stigmatization were a veritable elixir of life.

Disgust toward women's bodies (menstrual fluids, loose flesh) combines with fear and desire in a unique way, so let's postpone that topic.

If it is crazy and doomed to think that we can really avoid contact with animality, it is not so crazy to think that we can avoid contact with members of those symbolically freighted subgroups. Shakespeare's England simply expelled the Jews, so there simply were no Jews in Britain between 1290 and 1656. It was a brilliant stroke on the part of Shakespeare and his peers to imagine the disgusting in the form of a group that was real, that could be historically chronicled and vividly imagined, but that simply was not present in Britain at all. In our own time, the Nazi attempt to exterminate all the Jews of Europe was seriously undertaken and to a horrible extent successful. People with disabilities and aging people have also been targeted for extermination, but, much more often, they have simply been pushed to the margins, removed from the public square. (Many cities used to have "ugly laws" forbidding people with disabilities or upsetting appearances from appearing in public space.[14]) Gays and lesbians were forced to live closeted lives, presenting in public only those aspects of themselves that fit in with the norms of the dominant group. In a wide range of cases, then, projective disgust makes people hide or retreat.

In other cases, the disgust-group is found useful by the dominant group, so they don't want to get rid of its presence completely. Then elaborate rituals develop to police interactions and prevent contamination. The Indian caste hierarchy, American treatment of African Americans, and male treatment of women all belong to this type: they are seen all the time, doing their useful work, but arrangements prevent contamination. And people more or less come to believe that by avoiding X and Y and Z they really do avoid sweat and feces and semen and snot. If an African American doesn't swim in a public pool, that somehow means that the pool is clean, no feces or sweat or urine there! (Rationalizers said that these groups carried STDs or other contagious diseases, and many probably really did believe this.)

What about moralized disgust? It's a familiar phenomenon that people feel disgust at things that they also think immoral.

[14]See Susan M. Schweik, *The Ugly Laws: Disability in Public* (New York: NYU Press, 2010). Chicago used to have such a law, and a former colleague of mine with a major neurological disability, one of this country's most brilliant younger scholars of constitutional law, used to point out that under those laws he would not have been permitted to appear in public.

In some of these cases, the aversion has two components that we can at least try to separate. Thus, many people think homosexual sex immoral without feeling disgust, and many feel that gay sex is "yucky" without subscribing to a particular moral argument. Some people feel disgust for the bodies of African Americans and also subscribe to arguments holding that African Americans tend to be criminals; but again, the two elements are often found apart from one another. More puzzling are cases where it looks as if the disgust itself directly targets the immorality: we can be disgusted at the corruption of politicians, at horrible crimes, or at racism and sexism themselves. This phenomenon has long puzzled researchers, and it has puzzled me. I've treated it at length in other work.[15] So let me summarize.

In some of these cases, people are just using words loosely: when they say, "These politicians disgust me," they are really expressing protest or anger, and their emotion probably isn't disgust. In some cases, it really is disgust, but the ideation, more closely inspected, focuses on typical disgust ideas: the criminal's bloody acts are vividly imagined; the politicians are imagined as like cockroaches or rats. In other cases, insofar as the emotion is disgust and not anger, there is still at its core a general idea of purity and dirt, and the person is expressing a wish to be free from the contamination of those dirty people, to get to a purer place. In my view, such cases do not show that disgust is socially constructive, since what the disgusted person wants to do is to flee, rather than to solve the problem. (I

[15]Hiding from Humanity, ch. 2.

sometimes imagine moving to Finland, a country I know pretty well but not too well, and therefore imagine as a land of blue clear lakes and social-democratic purity.) Nor is disgust reliable for legal purposes: thus, jurors are typically disgusted by the mention of blood and gore, but murders may be especially awful and not involve such sensory characteristics—consider the murder of a guard during a bank robbery. So, I resist the claim of some scholars that in such cases disgust is politically productive and reliable. But I grant that some of these cases don't involve the wish to subordinate.

DISGUST AND WHAT WE FEAR

Fear lies at the heart of primary disgust, keeping us away from what both alarms and (often) threatens us. Because primary disgust does not sufficiently distance us from what we dread, fear engineers projective disgust as a further protective mechanism, threatening equality and mutual respect. But because fear ramifies widely, creating many different varieties of disgust stigma, we need to understand the endless plasticity of these social formations in order to zero in on the ones most pertinent to our own political moment. Although we could focus on many types of exclusion, I want to focus on two that seem especially acute today: bodily disgust toward African Americans and toward gays, lesbians, and transgender people. (Complicated hate-filled reactions to the presence and success of women in our society involve a toxic brew of disgust, anger/blame, and envy, so I'll discuss them separately.)

Let me mention briefly what this chapter does not include.

The disgust that fuels discrimination on grounds of disability and age is an important social evil, but I have just focused attention on it in my coauthored book *Aging Thoughtfully*,[16] so I shall leave that to one side. In any case, it does not seem to be an issue involved in our current debates: age discrimination, I'm afraid, is robustly universal and crosses party lines. Muslims are targeted for hate crimes, and in India, the propaganda whipping up that animosity does use a rhetoric of disgust, speaking of Muslim bodies as smelly (because they allegedly eat beef), hypersexual, and hyperfertile, by contrast to the allegedly pure and sexually self-controlled body of the Hindu. Narendra Modi campaigned in his home state of Gujarat on the slogan, "We are two and we have two [each Hindu couple has two children]; they are five [because each Muslim man is imagined as having four wives, even though polygamy is no more common among Muslims than among Hindus], and they have twenty-five [just a nice number to make the rhyme work]." Using obscene propaganda about Muslim women's bodies, Modi and his allied groups whipped up murderous rage against Muslims, leading to the Gujarat genocide of 2002, in which around two thousand innocent Muslim civilians were murdered.[17] But in the US the hatred of Muslims is focused on Muslims as objects of fear, without disgust.

[16]Martha C. Nussbaum and Saul Levmore, *Aging Thoughtfully: Conversations About Retirement, Romance, Wrinkles and Regret* (New York: Oxford University Press, 2017).

[17]I discuss this appalling and hideous set of crimes in my *The Clash Within: Democracy, Religious Violence, and India's Future* (Cambridge, MA: Harvard University Press, 2007).

Let's then test the analysis by focusing on my two test cases. They help us see how the damage of disgust can be inhibited through education and law.

In our recent Jim Crow era, which has not entirely disappeared, African American bodies were regarded with disgust, as sources of contamination. Drinking fountains, lunch counters, swimming pools, hotel beds—none of these could be shared. People otherwise intelligent and civilized believed that black bodies carried a powerful taint. As a child of a racist father from the Deep South (though living in the North), I was told that African Americans smelled different, that they would spread disease by using the same toilet facilities, that if they used a drinking glass, you had better not drink from that glass again, even after washing it. Although this disgust was based in fantasy, it took on bodily reality: thus, during Reconstruction one hears of people who, having moved from the South to the North and then being seated at a mixed-race table, literally vomited.[18] I've used the past tense, optimistically. But the white supremacist marchers in Charlottesville in August 2017 show us that these ugly fantasies live on.

But what was this anxiety all about? In part this disgust evinces the anxiety about animality and embodiment that is common to all forms of disgust stigma. But each projective formation has its own specific traits, and we can understand ours more clearly through two comparisons: to the disgust involved in the Indian caste hierarchy and to anti-Semitic disgust.

[18]Conversation with Jane Dailey, historian at University of Chicago, who is writing a book on this period.

The Indian attitude toward "untouchables" shared (and, sadly, still shares, all too often, since 30 percent of Hindu households still observe untouchability) many themes with our own racial disgust. These include a refusal to share drinking water and food, swimming pools, hotel beds, and a more general avoidance of bodily contact. B. R. Ambedkar, the great architect of the Indian Constitution and one of the top legal minds of the modern era, grew up, he tells us, as a *dalit* (formerly called "untouchable") child who was rich and well fed and clothed—because his father worked for the British army, which was racist in many respects but did not observe the caste hierarchy. At school he could not drink water from the common tap (in a region of India where the temperature often reaches 115 degrees) or sit on the mats on which other children sat. When he traveled with his sisters, wearing expensive clothes, neat and starched, and carrying lots of cash, he could find no hotel that would take them.

All of this sounds just like the Jim Crow South, where even well-to-do and successful black baseball players could not stay at "white" hotels, well into the mid-1950s.[19]

But there are differences. Here's a weird difference that just goes to show how irrational the whole disgust system is. African Americans often cooked and served food in white households. A *dalit*, however, could never even enter the kitchen in an upper-caste Hindu household, and the touching of food was a central locus of stigma.[20] There's a further weirdness,

[19]See Hank Aaron, *I Had a Hammer: The Hank Aaron Story* (New York: Harper, 1991).

[20]Thus, in Indian philosopher Rabindranath Tagore's great novel *Gora*

however: in the Jim Crow South, often the plates off which black people had eaten were broken so that they could not be used again. Baseball great Hank Aaron describes this common practice in his autobiography, noting, "If dogs had eaten off those plates, they'd have washed them."[21] So the US South had convoluted and bizarre practices regarding food: blacks could cook and serve food for whites, but they were thought to contaminate the plates they themselves used.

And here's a further, large difference between Indian caste disgust and US racism: *Dalit* men were regarded as pathetic, weak, and low; they were not seen as fearful sexual predators who desired sex with upper-caste women. Avoidance of sexual contact went along with the whole system, but rape by *dalit* men was not a fear central to upper-caste ideation. We could say that the *dalit* man was seen as rather like a cockroach: dirty, low, disgusting, but not really powerful or strong.

It was otherwise with the African American male. An honest look at our heated debates about school integration in the 1950s shows that the fear of sexual contact between black men

---

(1910), the hero refuses to eat food cooked in his own mother's kitchen because she employs a Christian woman as a cook. (Christians were usually converts from the lower castes, so this issue is present as well.) He fantasizes a return to pure upper-caste Hinduism, as the way forward for India. But the title tells the story: early in the novel we learn that Gora, whose name means "Paleface," is actually the child of an Irish woman who died in the 1857 rebellion against the British army; Gora's mother has adopted the child out of compassion. So, Gora can never be an upper-caste Hindu, caste being transmitted by birth. His anguished discovery of his own origins prompts introspection and, eventually, a change of heart: India's future lies in accepting the equal humanity of all her people.

[21]Ibid., 47.

and white women was at the very heart of the reluctance to integrate schools. In a recent important article, my colleague Justin Driver, a leading scholar of constitutional law, has assembled all the evidence for this picture in a relentless manner, showing that even an apparently benign leader like Dwight Eisenhower was phobic on this topic.[22] Speaking confidentially to Chief Justice Earl Warren, then deciding *Brown v. Board of Education*, Eisenhower implored Warren to see that segregationist white Southerners "are not bad people. All they are concerned about is to see that their sweet little girls are not required to sit in school alongside some big black bucks."[23] The idea of the black man as a dangerous animal lying in wait ran through all of our fraught debates—and I would argue that these same images are potent now, though in many cases they have gone underground, fueling what psychologists call "implicit bias"—bias that shows up on empirical tests, even though the biased person is not aware of having it.[24] So disgust and fear combine in a way that is *sui generis* and quite different from the way disgust was shaped in India. Baseball great Don Newcombe tells the story of one all-white hotel that allowed the black ballplayers to stay, in 1954, so long as they promised

[22]Justin Driver, "Of Big Black Bucks and Golden-Haired Little Girls: How Fear of Miscegenation Informed *Brown v. Board of Education* and Its Resistance," forthcoming in *The Empire of Disgust.*

[23]Bernard Schwartz, *Super Chief: Earl Warren and His Supreme Court* (New York: New York University Press, 1983), 113, quoted in Driver, 64.

[24]The literature on implicit bias is huge by now, and empirically very convincing. A good summary is Mahzarin R. Banaji and Anthony G. Greenwald, *Blindspot: Hidden Biases of Good People* (New York: Random House, 2013).

not to use the swimming pool, in proximity to scantily clad white women—and they were given rooms that faced away from the pool![25] Seventy years later, these ideas haven't disappeared. In Charlottesville, Virginia, during the August 2017 white supremacist march, one young female counter-protester was told by a marcher (female), "'I hope you get raped by a nigger.'"[26]

Let's think now about Jews. Jews, like African Americans, were widely regarded, in both Europe and the US, as hyper-bodily and hyper-animal, as more smelly, more sexual, than their gentile counterparts. The Jewish nose was an obsessive topic of comment, and was clearly seen as a kind of genital organ. The trope that Jews smoke big long cigars (which my father repeated to me on many occasions) reinforced the picture of Jews as sensuous and indulgent.[27] (American anti-Semitism has similar themes. Today these too are rarely voiced, although the alt-right defiantly does so.) However, there were two large differences between anti-Semitic disgust and the racial disgust of that same era. First, Jews were seen as highly intelligent animals, dangerous because of their guile, whereas African American men were imagined as brute beasts. So, what bigots feared was subtly different: being taken

[25]Newcombe, quoted in Aaron, 124.

[26]https://www.nytimes.com/2017/08/13/opinion/university-virginia-uva-protests-charlottesville.html.

[27]See my "Jewish Men, Jewish Lawyers: Roth's 'Eli, the Fanatic' and the Question of Jewish Masculinity in American Law," in Saul Levmore and Martha C. Nussbaum, eds., *American Guy: Masculinity in American Law and Literature* (New York: Oxford University Press, 2014), 165–201.

over by a clever conspiracy of bankers in the former case, rape and murder in the latter. This shaped the parameters of the prejudice. Thus, my father objected strenuously to my appearing in public in a mixed-race group—apparently reasoning that people who saw such a group would suspect sexual intimacy. (What else, he evidently imagined people thinking, would a black man be doing there?) But he had no analogous fear of my socializing with Jews, so long as I was not going to marry one (as I later did), probably because he knew that people could infer all kinds of intellectual and professional purposes from such a gathering. Furthermore, although Jews were seen as hypersexual, they were not typically seen as rapists or predators or as physically aggressive. Indeed, more often Jewish skill in sports was denigrated and Jews were represented as weak.[28] So, here again we see that each disgust formation has its own nuances and its own history. The fact of common threads running through all forms is significant, but it doesn't relieve us of the responsibility of dissecting our own moment and our own pathologies.

These comparisons teach us that where Jews are concerned, insofar as we still sadly grapple with anti-Semitism in our time, what we need to watch out for are fantasies of Jewish guile, Jewish corruption, Jewish plots, as well as Jewish vulgarity and crudeness. Where African Americans are concerned, we need to watch out for the tendency to portray black men as predators, criminals, brutes, and violent by nature. And we also

[28]Hence the Jewish athletic star "Swede" Levov, of Philip Roth's *American Pastoral*, is viewed, and views himself, as an ethnic hybrid, an anomaly, a "Swede."

need to watch out for the idea that black children can't learn, or won't learn, or, even worse, that they will inevitably prefer crime to education. (Hank Aaron notes with some bitterness that reporters typically represented his reserved and shy demeanor as that of a "shuffling colored boy." They knew the story they were going to write before they met him.[29]) Given the strong psychological evidence that bias remains buried in most Americans' minds, even when we believe in all good faith that we are not racist, we must work extra hard in the opposite direction.

Thus, when decisions are made about school budgets, about school bussing, and about how to improve failing inner-city schools, whites, Asian Americans, and Latinos urgently need to work against their own likely implicit bias (and of course some blacks may share these biases), proceeding on the assumption that all children have similar capacities for learning and achievement in decent circumstances, and making extra efforts to give such circumstances to black children, emphasizing throughout the education process their future opportunities and possibilities. Chicago mayor Rahm Emmanuel has suggested recently that Chicago might adopt as part of high school graduation requirements a plan for each student's future, worked out in consultation with teachers and guidance counselors.[30] Children need to know what employment opportunities they have; they need to know that community colleges are free of charge and that attending one can open up many

[29]Aaron, 153–4,

[30]http://www.chicagotribune.com/news/local/politics/ct-rahm-emanuel-high-school-requirement-met-20170405-story.html.

future possibilities. Obviously, privileged kids already have this information, but requiring a plan is a way of making sure that teachers and guidance counselors don't let implicit bias lead them to shortchange African Americans on the assumption that they don't want to achieve or work.

In criminal justice, the history of bias carries a strong warning. Knowing that both police and civilians may harbor implicit pictures of black men as predators (and it is hardly ruled out that black police officers may also have implicit biases), we ought to favor police training that instructs officers about the studies that show high levels of implicit bias, and we should urge them to test themselves for such biases. Training should also place a large emphasis on procedural justice, as leading criminal justice scholars Tom Tyler and Tracey Meares of Yale Law School have been arguing. Firm procedural rules help disable bias and stigma.[31] Hank Aaron says that he dealt with the race bias of umpires, which he had long observed, by hitting more home runs than anyone else, thus not putting "my fate in the hands of the umpire."[32] But less extraordinary mortals can't always hit a home run: they have to rely on "the white man's justice," as Aaron puts it. We'd better work to make that justice a lot more truly just. Law has already done a lot to inhibit stigma: desegregating schools, rendering racial discrimination in housing and employment illegal, and integrating public facilities. There is more work to be done on the integration front, since many neighborhoods and many public schools are

[31]See https://trustandjustice.org/resources/intervention/procedural-justice.

[32]Aaron, 145.

de facto segregated. In her important book *The Imperative of Integration*, philosopher Elizabeth Anderson argues cogently that only integration of schools and housing will really put an end to stigma.[33] My analysis supports her: disgust feeds on fantasies of the other, and sharing a common daily life is the best way to explode these fantasies.[34]

Now let's turn to gays, lesbians, and transgender people. Here again, there is a thread of bodily disgust running throughout the political propaganda against equal rights, which bears a strong similarity to other instances of projective disgust. I was present in a Denver courtroom in 1994, during the bench trial of the case that later became the landmark Supreme Court case *Romer v. Evans*, on the day when Will Perkins, chief proponent of a referendum known as Amendment 2 that had denied gays and lesbians the right to seek protection from local antidiscrimination ordinances, testified. He admitted that in support of the referendum he had circulated pamphlets that said that gay men eat feces and drink "raw blood." Fifteen years later, writing about constitutional law and same-sex rights, I studied the pamphlet literature circulated in the early twenty-first century by opponents of gay civil rights and found that little had changed. Here's a typical example, from a pamphlet by Paul Cameron (a leading anti-gay activist) entitled *Medical Consequences of What Homosexuals Do*:

[33]Elizabeth S. Anderson, *The Imperative of Integration* (Princeton: Princeton University Press, 2010).

[34]A very important study in this area is Glenn Loury, *The Anatomy of Racial Inequality* (Cambridge, MA: Harvard University Press, 2002).

> The typical sexual practices of homosexuals are a medical horror story—imagine exchanging saliva, feces, semen and/or blood with dozens of different men each year. Imagine drinking urine, ingesting feces and experiencing rectal trauma on a regular basis. Often these encounters occur while the participants are drunk, high, and/or in an orgy setting. Further, many of them occur in extremely unsanitary places (bathrooms, dirty peep shows), or, because homosexuals travel so frequently, in other parts of the world.
>
> Every year, a quarter or more of homosexuals visit another country. Fresh American germs get taken to Europe, Africa, and Asia. And fresh pathogens from these continents come here. Foreign homosexuals regularly visit the US and participate in this biological swapmeet.[35]

To the canonical references to bodily fluids and dirty surroundings, Cameron adds the idea of foreign travel as source of contamination, surely an idea that resonates with many Americans.

Okay, let's now step back and analyze this specific case of projective disgust. First of all, it is not aimed at achieving total separation of facilities, for the obvious reason that this would be impossible to police, given the closet. Second, the disgust formation has little to do with a general aversion to same-sex conduct as such, since women are standardly omitted from disgust propaganda and sex between two women is

[35]Pamphlet, accessed 2009. Cameron's views are further discussed in *From Disgust to Humanity*.

a titillating staple of pornography directed at straight men. (In Britain, sex between two women was never illegal. In the US it often was, but it's fair to say that hate literature gave this option short shrift.) The propaganda is also, obviously, not directed at preventing gay men from having sex with and marrying women. Indeed, that would be a "good" outcome for the anti-gay movement. The propaganda depicts gay men as rapacious and sex-crazed, but not as threatening to our "sweet little girls." Indeed, the bigot wishes they would take a greater interest in those girls, and sexual orientation "conversion therapy," though discredited, continues to attract support. However, gay men are indeed seen as potential predators—toward straight men, as America's agonized debates about shared showers in the military showed. The very gaze of a gay man was seen as deeply threatening.

One sometimes hears of another anxiety: that by getting married to one another, gay people would somehow "sully" or "taint" the marriages of the heterosexuals who live next door. Such an idea, however, cannot be understood without thinking in terms of irrational ideas of stigma and contamination. (It can't really be a consistent moral thought, since the people who express it are content with laws permitting criminals and even child abusers to marry.)

What's really going on here? People may, of course, have personal moral objections to homosexual contact or to same-sex marriages; but this would naturally lead them to avoid such contact and such marriages, to counsel their children against them, and to join religious groups that share their beliefs. That's how people typically deal with their moral objections to other types of immorality, such as financial corruption or failure to meet financial obligations. Such moral objections do not explain the anxiety and disgust with which sexual orientation and gender identity have been discussed. Many Jews and Christians do not approve of interreligious marriages, and they counsel their children against them. But there's no disgust there—unless there is antecedent anti-Semitic or racial disgust. So why does the idea of same-sex marriage arouse disgust? It seems that the projective disgust targeting gay men in particular, and LGBT people more generally, is partly a general disgust anxiety about bodily fluids and sexuality. Gay men, because their sex is non-procreative, seem somehow more sexual than other people (most of whose sexual acts are also, of course, non-procreative), and they come to emblematize the fears many Americans have about the uncontrollable "animal" nature of bodily desire. In part, too, this disgust is an anxiety about the "new," the uncannily unconventional. In times of upheaval and moral and cultural change, people need to draw sharp lines and to repudiate anything that diverges from previously accepted patterns.

Today, at a time when gays and lesbians are living productive lives in every region of our country, dispelling disgust by their sheer presence and their constructive engagement in communities of many kinds, a new object of disgust anxiety has surged into prominence: trans people who want to use the bathroom of their chosen gender. It's too soon to have good studies of how projective disgust figures in these phenomena, but it is surely significant that the bathroom is their focal point. And the fact that the anxieties make no sense is a good sign that they come from some other and deeper place. Why do I say that they don't make sense? Because a person who looks like a female would not upset people by entering a women's room, where the other women would have no way at all of seeing their genital anatomy. She would look just like them, as is her intention and commitment. It would be a person who looks exactly like a male who might make women anxious in the women's room, and yet it is exactly this situation that anti-trans activists want to require by law: a person who has transitioned from female to male would be forced to use the women's room.

This case, then, resembles the anti-gay animus already discussed: it involves a fear of change, a desire to enforce traditional boundaries, and a bodily shrinking from vulnerable people that is either an instance of projective disgust or is closely akin to it. It is utterly different from a religious or even moral objection.

All my three cases involve disgust, but not the simple type of disgust with which one tries to avoid slugs or roaches. Disgust becomes dangerous in these cases, prompting opposition to equal civil rights, or even crimes of bias, because of an underlying fear (of bodies, of animality, and of change itself) that feeds the disgust.

WHY DISGUST NOW?

Either hate crimes have really increased or more of them are being reported. In either case, there's new awareness of this social problem. In part this greater concern may be occasioned by signals from the newly influential alt-right, which has a permissive attitude toward bias and indeed doesn't even see it as such. Demeaning stereotypes that were long carefully hidden parade openly in 2017 on the streets of Charlottesville. In part, there may be a subtly different explanation. In studying violence against lesbians and gay men, Gary David Comstock found that the cause for this choice of target was not a deep-seated hatred, but simply the belief (often on the part of drunken youths seeking to act out and create trouble) that the police didn't care about these people and thus one could assail them with impunity.[36] So the influence of the alt-right might be operating in a slightly different way, signaling to potential aggressors a relaxing of public protections for vulnerable groups. They are people against whom one may be able to aggress with impunity. President Trump's failure to condemn bias groups unequivocally is thus extremely dangerous. Our understanding of implicit bias, peer pressure, and "cascades" suggests that hatred is labile. Most people who engage in hate marches and even hate crimes do not have a lifelong commitment to such actions; they can go either way and can be "radicalized" by signs of permission and approval. In any case, we have plenty of evidence now that bias crimes are a large social problem, and that our proclaimed "postracial" era has not yet arrived.

However, my account of disgust, linking it to fear of the stickiness and vulnerability of embodiment, suggests an additional diagnosis for an upsurge of bias. When people feel very

[36]Gary David Comstock, *Violence Against Lesbians and Gay Men* (New York: Columbia University Press, reprint ed. 1995).

insecure, they lash out to blame and scapegoat the vulnerable. We can now add that their tendency to project disgust outward is likely to rise to the extent that their own sense of bodily vulnerability and mortality rises. Disgust is always specific, combined with specific fear-thoughts. But the insight that disgust is about fear and fueled by a constellation of specific fears makes it plausible that the need for a disgust-group and the intensity of disgust-stigma will rise, other things equal, in times of general insecurity. Being aware of this phenomenon should make us redouble our efforts to scrutinize our politics for hidden and not-so-hidden bias.

What about positive efforts to counter disgust and stigma? Walt Whitman's proposal that we should celebrate our own bodies, and, thence, "the likes of them" in other men and women, is utopian. Does it suggest any strategy for democracy to follow? Clearly the war against disgust must be fought first of all in the family, in the school, and in the upbringing of children more generally. School integration across all the problematic axes of difference goes a long way to assist people in seeing different bodies as non-monstrous and fully human—but only if schools and teachers monitor bullying and cultivate an atmosphere of inclusiveness and respect. I have already suggested that where race is concerned, real integration of housing and schools is an urgent necessity. The fact that gay, lesbian, and transgender children can turn up in any family means that the task of integration is less complicated. Basically, it requires encouraging young people to "come out" to family and classmates, and the fact that so many have already done so is surely a big part of the sweeping and highly age-related social change we have seen on topics such as same-sex marriage and bathrooms.

But children are not innocent of bias by the time they are in school, and efforts to stamp out bullying and stigmatization of children by one another are crucial parts of any successful integration program. Today's Internet and social media present many dangers, since people can access hate groups very easily and avoid contact with more positive messages. Fortunately, television and film offer better possibilities. Comedy is a particularly valuable anti-disgust genre because, ever since Aristophanes, comedy has pursued an agenda of reconciliation with the body. If you can laugh at the ridiculous things bodies do, it becomes that much harder to view the bodies of minorities with anxiety.

Thus, people who thought they didn't know any gays or lesbians can become the virtual friends of Will, Grace, Karen, and Jack, learning that gay men pursue different paths, that they can be loving friends to women (better, often, than straight men), and that they are not aiming at the disintegration of society. (Even Jack, who pursues pleasure, loves his son.) Or they can recognize, watching *Modern Family*, the truth that families are multiform, that same-sex couples care for children, that love, resilience, and humor are more important than the traditional or untraditional nature of their trappings. Race needs tragedies as well as comedies at this point in our social evolution, and most of the high-quality shows are not mendaciously neat like the *Cosby Show*, but run the gamut between tragedy and comedy: *The Wire*, *Orange Is the New Black*, and feature films such as the Oscar-winning *Moonlight*, which brings our two types of exclusion together. Hollywood has done far better with sexual orientation than with race up until now, but things are at least starting to change.

It seems perverse to consider cutting federal funding for the arts and humanities, when we understand their role in bringing people together across divisions often made worse by social media. Really, and this is the heart of the matter, such mass media can bring us together with ourselves.

5

ENVY'S EMPIRE

So far, we've seen how primary fear interacts with two developmentally later emotions, anger and disgust. Fear often hijacks the sense of outrage and protest, turning it into a toxic desire for payback. And fear infuses disgust's aversion to mortality and embodiment, producing strategies that exclude and subordinate. Now we must add another emotion to the poisonous brew: envy. Envy is at large in our nation.

Envy has threatened democracies ever since they began to exist. Under absolute monarchy and especially under feudalism, people's possibilities were fixed, and they might easily believe that fate, or divine justice, had placed them where they were. But a society that eschews fixed orders and destinies in favor of mobility and competition opens the door wide to envy for the competitive achievements of others. If envy is sufficiently widespread, it can eventually threaten political stability—particularly when a society has committed itself to "life, liberty, and the pursuit of happiness" for all. Envy says that only some enjoy the good things of life. Enviers hate those people and want to destroy their happiness.

We see envy on both the "right" and the "left." On the right, a sense of stagnation, helplessness, and even despair propels many lower-middle-class people into envious denigration of Washington elites, of mainstream media, of successful minorities, of women taking "their jobs." People wish ill to those by whom they feel eclipsed, or displaced, or neglected. On the left, many have-nots envy the power of bankers, of big business, and of political insiders who support those interests. Envy is not simply critique (which is always valuable), since it involves animus and destructive wishes: it wants to spoil the enjoyment of the "haves."

Let me say right away that I view envy as problematic even when its cause is just. In many current cases, it's difficult to figure out where justice lies. There is surely merit in the grievances of working-class white people, just as there is merit in the demands of the left for greater economic justice. But it's one thing to say, "Here is a problem we need to solve, and you should join with us in figuring out a better way." It's quite another thing to wish ill to the dominant group and to want to spoil their happiness. Envy's hostile desire, like (and closely related to) the retributive element in anger, is a bad thing for democracy even when the envied don't have a right to all the good things they enjoy. Envy leads to a picture of social cooperation as a zero-sum game: for me to enjoy the good life, I have to make you unhappy. This type of thinking is similar to, and very likely rooted in, envy between siblings: the envious sibling doesn't just want love and attention, she wants to *displace* the other one *from* love and attention, just as, for Aaron Burr in Lin-Manuel Miranda's *Hamilton*, putting himself into "the room where it happens" requires evicting his rival. Even if the sibling's parents (or Burr's quasi-parent, George Washington) had been unfair in lavishing attention on the rival sibling (Hamilton), it is always unsavory to wish pain and failure to the other as a condition of one's own success. But this is a hard lesson to learn, since democracy, to some extent unlike family, is inherently competitive. Can it arrange to have competition without envy?

DEFINING ENVY

What, then, is envy? As usual, philosophers typically ask about definitions, and this search for clarity proves useful, directing us to the root of this insidious political problem. People say different things in different times and places—but there's a common core of agreement.

Envy is a painful emotion that focuses on the advantages of others, comparing one's own situation unfavorably to theirs. It involves a rival (this could be a group) and a good or goods the envier thinks very important. Enviers are pained because the rival has those good things and they do not. Typically envy involves hostility toward the fortunate rival: the envier wants what the rival has and feels ill will toward the rival in consequence. Envy thus creates animosity and tension at the heart of society, and this hostility may ultimately prevent society from achieving some of its goals.

Now we need to distinguish envy from three of its cousins. One cousin is *emulation*. Emulation also involves a focus on the advantages of others, and it also involves important matters. But people who emulate feel no ill will: they view those others as outstanding exemplars. They don't want to take anything away from those people; they just want to move closer themselves. What's the difference? Two related things, it seems. Emulators think that they can indeed move closer to the goal. For example, by following the advice of a beloved teacher they can become more like that teacher. And second, very important, emulation focuses on achievements that are not entirely matters of zero-sum competition. The reason students think that they can move closer to their teacher is that they believe many people can have knowledge, and the teacher's knowledge does not threaten them, but actually assists them. Or think about kindness. It would be weird to envy your friend because she is so kind. Just be that way! Work on yourself! When the quality is one that we think people can attain by effort, emulation is far more likely than envy.

Envy is different. Its ill will typically comes from a feeling of impotence, which I'll later connect to primary fear. There's no obvious way of getting what the rival has, and enviers feel doomed to the inferiority that they experience. Often, furthermore, this sense of doom is linked to the fact that some things are not wide open to anyone who tries to get them. Being popular, being rich, winning an election—all these are examples of competitive, zero-sum goods: goods in short supply, where one person's possession threatens another person's chances.

Another cousin of envy is *jealousy*. At first the two might seem almost the same, but they are importantly different. Both envy and jealousy involve hostility toward a rival with regard to the possession or enjoyment of a valued good. Jealousy, however, is typically about fear of losing something one has—usually a relationship of personal love and attention. Whereas envy senses the absence of good, jealousy focuses on its valued but unstable presence. Because jealousy focuses on the self's most cherished relationships, it can often be satisfied, as when it becomes clear that the rival is no longer a competitor for the affections of the loved person, or was never a real competitor. Only pathological jealousy keeps inventing new and often imaginary rivals, and jealousy is not always pathological.

Envy, by contrast, is rarely satisfied, because the goods on which it typically focuses (status, wealth, fame, other competitive goods) are unevenly distributed in all societies, and no person can really count on having more than others. When we're insecure, we feel that we may not get the things that we need in order to live well. But what is distinctive of envy is the fantasy that others have the good things and I do not: I am on the outside of a happy relationship, a happy job, a happy social life.

Think of Othello and Iago. Othello was jealous, and pathologically so, obsessed with the fantasized disloyalty of Desdemona. Most spouses are not like this. But he did not have a general insecurity about status or success, or feel cut off from wonderful things that were just out of reach. Iago, by contrast, is not jealous of Othello: he doesn't crave Othello's love and attention. What he wants is to be Othello, to have the good things Othello has: fame, achievement, love. He sees that he doesn't have those things, so he wants to spoil the happiness of Othello, to render him loveless, low, miserable.

Finally, perhaps the most difficult distinction of the three, envy is a cousin of the type of anger that is based on belief in a status-injury. Envy does indeed focus on status: the rival has good things and I do not. Like anger, it is accompanied by hostile feelings toward the rival. The primary difference is that status-anger requires a belief that some definite insult or affront has occurred; envy, by contrast, feeds on the rival's happiness alone: the rival may have done nothing to insult the envier, and indeed may not even be aware of the envier's existence. This distinction is important but difficult to make in any particular case, because enviers like to fantasize insult and to blame the happy, even when blame isn't justified. Even more subtly, they may blame the rival by blaming a social hierarchy in which the rival has a privileged place (whether or not that structure is in fact unfair or demeaning). Once again: critique is always legitimate, but envy is not simply critique, it is destructive hostility.

ENVY'S ROOTS IN FEAR

I've said that envy is born of insecurity. Fear, then, is at its root: the fear of not having what one desperately needs to have. If we were complete, we would not need anything, and so we would not have envy. Or if, being incomplete, we were nonetheless confident in our ability to grab hold of what we need, then the fact that others have good things would not be an emotional problem. So, we need to think about insecurity and helplessness to understand envy's power.

To see why it's so important to link envy to fear, let's consider a powerful view of envy that does not make that connection: the view of Immanuel Kant. According to Kant, human life contains "radical evil": a propensity to harm others that is not learned in culture, but is part of our human situation itself. However, the problem is not that the devil drives us or that we have an innate evil spirit. We are basically oriented toward goodness. The problem is that other people get in the way:

> Envy, addiction to power, avarice, and the malignant inclinations associated with these, assail his nature, which on its own is undemanding, *as soon as he is among human beings.* Nor is it necessary to assume that these are sunk into evil and are examples that lead him astray; it suffices that they are there, that they surround him, and that they are human beings, and they will mutually corrupt each other's moral disposition and make one another evil.[1]

Kant's account rings true in some ways: envy does seem to arise as soon as people are in groups, or even families. But the story

[1]Kant, *Religion Within the Limits of Mere Reason* (1793), Cambridge Texts in the History of Philosophy, ed. and trans. Allen Wood and George di Giovanni (Cambridge: Cambridge University Press, 1999), Akademie 6.94 (these are the standard page numbers of the Berlin Academy edition, given in the margins of editions and translations).

is obviously incomplete. *Why* does this happen? Why does the mere presence of other people lead to competitive and hostile behavior? And does envy always arise in group situations? Surely some situations make destructive envy far more likely than others.

In his memorable discussion of envy in *A Theory of Justice*, John Rawls answers my second question.[2] He suggests that there are three conditions under which outbreaks of socially destructive envy are especially likely. First, there is a psychological condition: people lack secure confidence "in their own value and in their ability to do anything worthwhile." Second, there is a social condition: many circumstances arise when this psychological condition is experienced as painful and humiliating, because the conditions of social life make the discrepancies that give rise to envy highly visible. Third, the envious see their position as offering them no constructive alternative to mere hostility. The only relief they can envisage is to inflict pain on others.

This is an important analysis, offering us insight into our current predicament, as we'll see. Rawls, however, did not try to answer my first question: what is really at the bottom of the problem of envy? People can be loving and cooperative: so, it can't be right to say that the mere existence of a plurality ushers envy onto the scene.

The philosopher who got to the heart of the matter is—once again—Lucretius, who applied the general view of his

[2]John Rawls, *A Theory of Justice* (Cambridge, MA: Harvard University Press, 1971), 532–537.

mentor Epicurus to the problems of the Roman Republic, which was already a cauldron of destructive envy in his time (around 99–55 BCE), and which imploded shortly thereafter. Here's what Lucretius saw all around him:

> From a similar cause, from that very same fear,
> Envy wastes them away:
> Look how this man, before their very eyes, has power,
> How everyone gazes at that one, as he gets some distinguished honor –
> While they themselves (they complain) are wallowing in darkness and filth.
>
> (III.74–77)

This marvelous poetic account captures, I think, the peculiar pain of envy. Envious people are obsessed with looking at the successes of others; seeing those, they compare their lot unfavorably to theirs. Envy does make you feel as if you are in the dark, and also dirty, tainted, wallowing. Seeing yourself that way does waste or gnaw you away inside. This combination of hopelessness and sharp torment makes envy one of the most excruciating of the emotions.

Lucretius also tells us why we're so often at the mercy of this ugly emotion: it's all caused by "that very same fear," namely, what I've been calling infantile, or primary, fear. In other words, it is because of a deep underlying anxiety, a root-level painful insecurity, that people engage in zero-sum competition and hate the people who succeed. It's not, then, just the sheer presence of others, it's something deeper, something that assails us as soon as we are born into a world of neediness and powerlessness.

Lucretius, as we saw, has a particular view about primary fear that is not entirely right. He thinks that it is all about death, and that its power depends on nefarious religious entrepreneurs, who dupe us into thinking that death is terrifying, mostly by the threat of punishment in the afterlife. He thinks that without this interference, people would be insecure in many ways, but not unstably so. We have reason to doubt this reductive thesis. We fear all sorts of things because we are weak and powerless in all sorts of ways. Primary fear is manifold and operates in every area of life. When it is strong, groups of people can easily become cauldrons of envy.

Lucretius, perhaps the first (Western) theorist of the unconscious mind, held that primary fear operates beneath the level of consciousness, tainting everything with its "blackness." Envy's roots in fear are not evident to the tormented adult, but we can walk the causal chain backward and see how it typically arises, in an anxious sense that others have good things and we do not.

Melanie Klein, the greatest psychoanalytical theorist of envy, has a similar view. Klein constantly emphasizes that our adult world can be fully understood only by grasping its roots in infancy. She describes envy as rooted in a primary anxiety that one is separated from the good things—nourishment, love, gratification. "Early emotional life is characterized by a sense of losing and regaining the good object," and the anxiety that goes with this alternation between satiety and emptiness quickly becomes, as we saw, "persecutory," blaming the parent for withholding all the good things. Here's where envy kicks in. The Lucretian infant, feeling that pained sense of loss and abandonment, forms the idea that the parent is happy and complete and then wants to spoil that happiness. Klein may be a bit extreme when she says that the infant's fantasy is that of putting "bad excrements" into the parent to spoil and sully her, but if it's not a literal thought, it is certainly a powerful image of what we want when we envy someone.

Envy thus begins a vicious cycle. Wanting to attack and dirty the happy object—who is also loved—leads to feelings of guilt and badness, which make the infant feel all the more cast into outer darkness and removed from the happiness of love and attention.

Envy also bleeds into blame. Sometimes the envier thinks simply, *I really want what that person has.* But it is so easy to slide from that view into a related one: *I deserve those things, and they don't.* The politics of envy sometimes just says frankly, "We want what they [women, immigrants, elites] have." But people like to moralize their envy, and very often what begins as pure envy slides over to, *They are bad people, they don't deserve what they have.* This slide is an old story: classical scholar Robert Kaster has demonstrated that Roman envy (*invidia*) has the same two forms, moralized and non-moralized, and moves uneasily between them.[3] That's how

[3]Robert A. Kaster, *Emotion, Restraint, and Community in Ancient Rome* (New York: Oxford University Press, 2005), ch. 4, 84–103.

envy hitches its wagon to the politics of blame. Sometimes the "haves" really have done something unfair or insulting, and sometimes not.

Of course, a third possibility remains: the have-nots can make a reasoned critique of the personal wrongdoing or structural inequality that oppresses them and offer proposals for improvement. The spirit would be that of what I've called Transition-Anger, which is free from envy, since it has no interest in spoiling the enjoyment of the powerful, but will instead, as King notes, seek to work with them in a constructive spirit.

As life teaches us, and as Klein makes clear, envy takes many paths in individual lives—and her analysis fits surprisingly well with Rawls's social analysis. Envy will never disappear entirely. But if the growing child begins to feel confidence in herself and her own access to the good things of life, and if she sees constructive alternatives to her destructive wishes—alternatives involving generosity, creativity, and love—she may be more easily able to surmount the pain of envy. It will remain a temptation, but it won't poison life. Klein focuses on family differences, neglecting the social and political dimension. But it's obvious—and this was Rawls's point—that political communities can also do a lot to make envy a far less disturbing problem. They can create secure confidence in people, about themselves and their access to the good things in life. They can minimize occasions where the stimulus to envy will become unusually prominent. And they can give people constructive alternatives, involving generosity and love of others.

How on earth could this be done? As we approach envy in society, let's take a slight detour, investigating one social institution where envy often gets out of hand.

ENVY IN ACTION: HIGH SCHOOL

A typical large American high school is a veritable cauldron of envy. We've all been there; let's think back to that uneasy time. Adolescence is an especially vulnerable time of life. About to be separated from the womb of the family and to undergo a virtual second birth, being thrust into an uncertain and often hostile world, teenagers would be weird if they did feel secure. But insecurity is one thing, destructive envy another. What is it that makes envy run rampant in high schools? First, there's the obvious fact that high school cultures usually foreground achievements that are highly competitive and positional, such as popularity, sexual magnetism, and skill in sports. No adolescent really feels confident about these things, but it's made far worse by the fact that there are always those in-crowd kids who appear to have all the good things, while most people do not. Lucretius's lines describe well the horrible feeling of being chewed up by envy, seeing those people who are stared at, who have all the power, while kids on the outside come to see themselves as groping in the dark or wallowing in the mud. This envy produces real violence, as we know. But even in the vast majority of cases where it doesn't, it still produces painful tensions, dangerous depressions, and hostile relationships.

High schools are not all the same. There are at least a few

in which sports matter less and academic achievement more. But that's not much better, because the frenetic competition to get into top colleges poisons what might be the joy of learning. Ubiquitously, kids are competing for competitive preeminence, and most of them won't be at the top of the class. In my all-women school in a privileged suburb, I was a terrible athlete, but I cleaned up in the academic department. Many people didn't have an alternative track to success; those people hated the school and never attend reunions. They felt in outer darkness for popularity and honors and hated the school and the honored ones for inflicting that pain. (I know: I tried hard to convince some of them to attend our fiftieth reunion!) And let's remember that people who went to that school were already a privileged elite, secure in their expectation of some type of employment and social position. Most other high schools have far more and far more basic insecurities to contend with.

Thinking about Rawls's three criteria, what could the people in charge do to render the experience of going through adolescence in a high school less toxic? Much has to be done long before, in the family, but there are things our high schools can do. First of all, they can offer everyone help with their academic work and college preparation. I am delighted to see that my school today is different: it now offers assistance with learning disabilities and takes the general attitude that the job is to maximize each person's potential, rather than to rank and reward. Such assistance will be much more helpful to nonelite students, however, if our society does much better with the problem of unequal access to higher education. There are enough places in college for everyone, but money is a terrible obstacle for many. If everyone feels that by effort they can get into, and afford, a suitable college, this does a lot to decrease one type of zero-sum competition.

Schools can also foster other areas in which students can contribute, such as drama, music, and other arts, which are less zero-sum and more cooperative than sports, and which also help kids to express the emotional turmoil they are experiencing. I recently visited a high school for troubled teens, kids who had been expelled from other public high schools. And though the compassion of the impressive principal and a curriculum that included group therapy had done a lot to make a difference, convincing these kids that someone is listening, it was astonishing to me that the school had no arts curriculum at all, not even poetry. At my suggestion they did add creative writing, and I'm told it has helped a lot: kids now have an outlet for their tumultuous emotions. But ignoring theater and dance still seems problematic. In my own high school, lots of us found solace from sports in the warm and relatively unenvious emotional culture of theater, which became my passion and my home.

Lucretius was talking about his own society, and the Roman Republic could certainly be compared to a large high school. Positional competition was everything. There was a sequence of honors, the *cursus honorum*, that every adult male had to embark on: succeed, or remain in outer darkness. Each office had age qualifications, and you had to go through them in order. It was reputationally crucial not only to get each of the offices in sequence—aedile, praetor, consul, proconsul—but to get them early, right after one became eligible. Otherwise the odor of failure hung around one ever after. That was bad enough, but how did one get those preferments? By election, but how did one manage that? By wealth, family honor, reputation, and personality-based campaigning. There was nothing like a law degree or a PhD, which one might attain by effort and hard work, thus displaying fitness to serve society. It really was just like high school, although money and family meant more, and sports meant less. A person like the great statesman Marcus Tullius Cicero, from an undistinguished, albeit wealthy, family, could attain prominence by being a skilled advocate for clients and by earning a lot of money. But not without great stress. Cicero's career was filled with what Klein calls "persecutory anxiety"—the feeling that his own access to the good things of Roman life was highly unstable, and that other people from distinguished old families had "his" place without any effort or distinction. So often in his letters and speeches, Cicero refers edgily to his own status as a "new man," that is, a family with no lofty history. And his bitter hatred of his rivals and enemies, though it sometimes has a real political justification, clearly derives at least part of its aggressiveness from envy, as Cicero dwells all too obviously on their attractiveness, their sexual conquests, their popularity.

This envy of attractive rivals sometimes led Cicero to unwise and excessive actions—such as his proposal for an illegal extrajudicial killing of the ringleaders in the Catilinarian conspiracy, which did much harm to his reputation. And his envy also often led him into unbalanced self-praise, as a kind of defense against rivals. This narcissistic tendency made him a joke to many and lessened his political effectiveness. Who could trust a man who wrote an epic poem about his own defeat of the Catilinarian conspiracy, with himself, of course, as the hero—a poem containing the oft-mocked line, "O Rome, fortunate to be alive during my consulship," "*O fortunatam natam me consule Romam.*" He was so eager to spoil his enemies and to proclaim his own merit that he didn't even notice the hideously unpoetic jingle that he put into the verse.

Cicero was a great man who made many contributions. But his mental life was made unstable by "persecutory aggression," and his contributions, great though they undoubtedly were, did less good to the state than they otherwise might have. And Cicero is the good case, a man who basically won his battle with envy and created much good. The same factors in Roman society that ate away at this patriotic man, turning him at times into a buffoon, also propelled worse people into power, people without high ideals or fine goals, people whose only interest was the positional game of rivalry, envy, and destruction. That (more or less) is how the Roman Republic, always deeply flawed, collapsed into tyranny. It's an example we should ponder.

ENVY AND DEMOCRACY: HAMILTON AND BURR

Let's now return to our own nation at its founding, where similar themes are prominent. American revolutionaries loved the Roman Republic and were virtually obsessed with its struggle against tyranny. They clearly had a lot of the same problems.

Envy and a destructive competition for honor and position were everywhere in our republic in its early days and did real harm. Some of the hostility took the form of status-based anger, as people took offense at insults of many types. Some of the hostility was pure envy with no real occasion for blame. The two could easily blur together: envious people were on the lookout for any putative insult, so that they could strike back through dueling.

But the Founders fared somewhat better than those ancient Romans. Despite living in a culture obsessed with competition for honor and status, they nonetheless struggled against envy, and to a surprising degree surmounted it. Love of the republic they were creating prevailed over destructiveness and hate.

Lin-Manuel Miranda's *Hamilton* is preoccupied, as we've seen, with anger based upon status-anxiety. It is also a meditation about the role of envy in the American founding and the importance of containing envy if we are to have a successful nation. The famous duel in which Burr kills Hamilton is its tragic climax, and the motif of dueling is woven throughout. In its contrast between Hamilton (ambitious but seeking good for the whole nation) and Burr (obsessed by envy, wanting to spoil Hamilton's success), the musical shows the dangers of fear-driven envy for democratic politics.

At its heart, *Hamilton* is about a choice of two possible political lives, the life of love and service to the new nation, and the life of fear-driven envy and zero-sum competition. The figures of Burr and Hamilton stand for alternative paths that individual members of the audience might follow. (It's not just about great leaders, then, it's about us all.)

Suppose a person, or a political group, chooses the path of rivalrous competition for glory. In that case, it will probably seem best not to have firm ideas or deep moral commitments, since it may be prudent to change course in accordance with prevailing fashion. That's Aaron Burr, charismatic and immensely able but unwilling to take a stand.[4]

Under Washington's wise tutelage, Hamilton learns that making a splash is easy, but creating something fine in politics is difficult and risky. ("Winning was easy," says Washington, "governing is harder.") Political creation, he learns, requires study, deliberation, maybe even philosophy! (All the Framers read at least Locke and Montesquieu, but Hamilton read far more.) And it involves risk and suffering. The reward is that you may be able to create something exceptional that lives on after you. Hamilton learns from Washington, but he really has made his choice from the start and needs only minor course correction. From his very first entrance he is already aiming to be both "a hero and a scholar," reading "every treatise on the shelf." And while Burr sings about his urgent desire to be inside that room, Hamilton is singing about creating something lasting and fine.

Things, however, are more complicated. For Hamilton can create what he creates only because he is also a relentless competitor. He always wants preeminence, and it's only because he gains it (winning Washington's regard and trust, for example) that he is able to leave a legacy to posterity.

In other words, attachment to worthy ideals is not sufficient

[4]The full text is given in the libretto in the CD.

for political creation. The aspiration to create something fine might be enough if you are trying to be virtuous in a family or a religious community; but the minute you enter a realm where the wherewithal to do good is in short supply, you have to play Burr's game, up to a point. If you're not in the room where it happens, you can't influence history's course. And you don't get to be in that room without successful competition against others. Whether we're talking about presidential candidates or less glamorous participants in the democratic process, creation and competition are very difficult to separate, and it's no surprise that pure idealists fall by the wayside in democratic politics. So, while Burr does not have to care about Hamilton's path, Hamilton is obliged to care, to some degree and instrumentally, about Burr's. Competition need not compromise virtue, but it always introduces temptations: slander, shading the truth, above all narcissism and lack of respect for others. In short, democracy is an uncertain fear-suffused realm in which nobody has space to unfold creative powers without the anxious pursuit of competitive advantage.

What's more, a drive for fame and public honor is probably an important ingredient in political creativity. At least we see that Hamilton's genuine ardor for ideas is always accompanied, and probably energized, by a desire to make a splash, which propels him past many obstacles. An illegitimate child and orphan, he has a thirst for success and recognition that accompany and feed his ardor for virtue and ideas. These acute insights complicate and deepen the central contrast.

Now we face the question: if political creation requires competition, does competition require envy? Or: to compete with my brother, do I have to want to spoil his enjoyment of the good things of life? To this all-important question, the musical gives the answer "no." Hamilton is proud and thirsty for honor, but almost entirely free of envy. Burr, like Iago, is utterly consumed by envy, and the play makes a strong case that envy is a cancer in the body politic that we should each resist individually and which we must reduce or extirpate as a nation.

Rawls spoke of three social conditions that make envy particularly dangerous. These conditions fit Miranda's Burr to a T. Some deep insecurity at his core (maybe connected to lacking a mother, since his died in his infancy) makes him obsessed with rivalrous competition. The conditions of social life in the new rough-and-tumble nation make everyone's position precarious. As for constructive alternatives: Burr, having attempted unsuccessfully to become close to Washington, having then attempted electoral politics without gaining the top office, finds nothing to fall back on other than hate. Envy begins in something specific: the desire to be at one particular secret meeting, to be "in the room where it happened." But quickly, within the compass of one song, it expands and becomes global: "I've got to be in the room where it happens."

The climax of the musical, and the Burr-Hamilton relationship, is the famous duel. In the musical, basically following history, Burr writes a provocative letter alluding to insults by Hamilton against his honor. Burr, then, represents his emotion as status-anger, with specific insults as its cause. However, by this time the audience is clear that the alleged insults are mere excuses for envious spoiling.

By this time in his life, at least, Hamilton firmly opposed

dueling on religious and moral grounds. He left a public statement describing his reason for accepting Burr's challenge despite those objections:

> All the considerations which constitute what men of the world denominate honor, impressed on me (as I thought) a peculiar necessity not to decline the call. The ability to be in future useful, whether in resisting mischief or effecting good, in those crises of our public affairs, which seem likely to happen, would probably be inseparable from a conformity with public prejudice in this particular.[5]

Miranda doesn't quote this fascinating text, but he narrates the duel in that spirit. In envy's empire, political virtue has to yield to envy's demands in order to act and make a difference. It doesn't have to be internally envious: but it has to live in a world where envy has great sway. Hamilton explained to many people that his solution to the dilemma was to accept the duel but throw away his shot, that is, deliberately shoot off-target, thus showing that he doesn't want to ruin Burr's life. Ironically, the man whose zeal for work and virtuous action makes him repeatedly proclaim, near the opening of the musical, "I'm not throwing away my shot," resolves to throw his shot away—which meant, as it turned out, throwing away the chance to work and create.

So they meet with their seconds out in New Jersey, where

[5]Hamilton, "Statement on Impending Duel with Aaron Burr," in *The Papers of Alexander Hamilton*, ed. Harold C. Syrett et al. (New York: Columbia University Press, 1961–87), 26:278.

anything goes. Hamilton shoots in the air. Burr, however, shoots to kill. To the extent that envy's malice rules society, virtue will often lose.

But America, it turns out, is not entirely envy's empire. In fact, Miranda represents Hamilton as a success, not a failure. Miranda's America is a split nation, but above all, it honors public-spirited and constructive achievement, and it doesn't like people who are above all naysayers, eager to spoil the achievements and the happiness of others. Dying, Hamilton wishes for a future in which others will sing his "song": and, of course, we are hearing it. Miranda himself (in the original cast run) is singing it. Hamilton has prevailed, because orphan, immigrant, he offers creative achievements that Miranda (and many before him) have found inspiring, have described, and have celebrated. In so many respects they are already in our nation and our lives: the US Constitution, with all its flaws, the financial system, the Federal Reserve Bank: apparently mundane matters that have been the backbone of our flawed yet still operating democracy.

The musical in the end makes a highly optimistic statement about American politics. We are beset by envious rivalry and destructive aggression. But in the end, we know where true good is located: in the love of our flawed nation, in the dedicated service of so many people, known and unknown, who are willing even to lay down their lives for democracy, in the determination to show that brotherhood, constructive work, and the inclusion of minorities and immigrants, shine brighter than hate. As advice to young people in today's United States, isn't this too naïve?

ENVY IN OUR POLITICAL MOMENT

Miranda is an optimist. But the ascendancy of fear in our politics makes optimism about envy difficult. There is a lot of Aaron Burr's spirit in America today. In Congress we so often see rivalry driven by envy's malice: one group wants to put down the policies of the other simply because they are or were preeminent, rather than engaging a common effort to create the best solution. More generally, in our lives as citizens we encounter all too much of Burr: people obsessed with insider standing, power, and status, and hating successful groups that appear to be "in the room where it happens." We don't fight duels with people who insult us, but we do much the same in different ways, insulting individuals and groups who seem to be our rivals, rather than listening to their arguments. And our president's memorable image of himself beating up CNN is an image right out of the honor-envy mania of the Founding, a spirit not conducive to good political deliberation.

Envious malice, as I've said, is not just on the right—though it is surely present there. On the left we find similar themes—in the hatred of "elites," "bankers," and "big business," even occasionally of "capitalism" itself, and in the desire not only to make the good things of life available to all but in the frequent desire to spoil or remove delight for those privileged ones. It is certainly possible to criticize the power of elites in our system without envy. But we all too often find, in place of rational critique, a purely negative desire to tear people down, rather than a determination to join, all of us together, to build a better society.

We even find Burr-like sentiments of violence and destruction. Otherwise admirable people are not exempt from this problem. On August 18, 2017, amid many excellent and dignified protests of President Trump's appallingly defective reactions to the white supremacist march in Charlottesville, economist and columnist Paul Krugman sounded an ugly and inappropriate note.[6] After comparing Donald Trump to the Roman emperor Caligula (a comparison surely far-fetched, since Caligula murdered many of his enemies, sometimes using horrendous tortures[7]), Krugman then concludes, "Finally, when his behavior became truly intolerable, Rome's elite did what the party now controlling Congress seems unable even to contemplate: It found a way to get rid of him." But it is well known that Caligula was assassinated by the Praetorian Guard (whose analog would be our Secret Service). Paul Krugman is an extremely intelligent and scholarly man. Given that this information is easily available on Wikipedia, the suggestion of assassination is either egregiously careless or deliberate. In neither case does it have a place in democratic discourse.

Krugman was reacting to envy with envy. The white supremacists who marched in Charlottesville (the immediate

[6]https://www.nytimes.com/2017/08/18/opinion/trump-caligula-republican-congress.html?action=click&pgtype=Homepage&clickSource=story-heading&module=opinion-c-col-right-region®ion=opinion-c-col-right-region&WT.nav=opinion-c-col-right-region.

[7]The comparison is reminiscent of the 1967 off-Broadway hit *MacBird*!, in which left-wing people, angry about the Vietnam War, compared Lyndon Johnson to Macbeth, suggesting that he was behind the murder of President Kennedy.

context for his column) were paradigms of the spirit of envy, expressing their wish to spoil the lives of those (Jews, African Americans) by whom they feel displaced: "You will not replace us; Jews will not replace us" was their cry. But it is dead wrong to counter this spirit of envy by more envious spoiling, even carelessly or inadvertently. The desire to spoil is always ugly, and uglier still when it fantasizes or suggests violence.

At the same time, our politics contains many Hamiltons, voices of hope and constructive effort, voices that speak with real love of the nation and its people. Sometimes it is difficult to hear these voices in the cacophony of insults and putdowns. Maybe Miranda has given us all a wake-up call: good ideas can come from anywhere—from immigrants (Hamilton) and even from bankers (also Hamilton). And in the wake of the national soul-searching that has followed the white supremacist violence in Charlottesville in August 2017, we have heard many eloquent statements about America that do indeed help us think forward—including many forceful statements from politicians of both parties, repudiating racism and urging brotherhood and inclusiveness. It's encouraging that former President Obama's tweet is now the most-liked tweet ever: "No one is born hating another person because of the color of his skin or his background or his religion. People must learn to hate, and if they can learn to hate, they can be taught to love, for love comes more naturally to the human heart than its opposite." Good words: now we need to put them into action.

TOWARD A POLITICS OF NON-ENVY

How can my analysis of envy help us in thinking our way forward? It helps us zero in on a challenge: how might our society create more Hamiltons and fewer Burrs—and political parties and institutions that are more Hamiltonian, seeking to solve problems constructively, than Burrian, seeking to put down and ruin others who threaten them. In a nation, as in a high school, it is possible to focus on helpful and public-spirited efforts, dignifying, praising, and rewarding Hamiltonian creative work, rather than the sort of zero-sum competition that was Burr's obsession. Our culture of fleeting celebrity and social media narcissism contributes to an envy culture. We need, instead, a culture of virtue and a conception of citizenship focused on virtue in the Hamilton sense: a high-minded yet realistic search for political solutions that unite.

This search has three levels: the personal, the social, and the institutional. They interact, since people's emotions respond to the institutions in which they live. And political institutions also have a large role to play in making people choose the Hamilton path, rejecting envy. One part of its role is to include: through nondiscrimination law, through respectful attention to previously excluded groups, a nation can make them feel that they have creative and constructive outlets for their talents. (That, at one level, is what *Hamilton* is all about, with its all-minority cast playing the Founders: let us have our shot and we won't waste it.)

Much of government's role, however, is structural. Let's think back to the Depression, a time when fear and insecurity dominated our national life in a way that outstrips anything we see today. The destitution that the economic collapse created, the searing misery of the Dust Bowl, families starving all across the nation—this is truly worse than anything happening now. Why? Because of the New Deal and its comprehensive assault on fear.[8] I believe that FDR was right on target when he said that we must fear fear itself, and when he said that the best antidote to the painful fear he saw all around him was to construct a basic social safety net that would make people able to rely on a social minimum in times of hardship. The "second bill of rights" that he sought to add to the existing civil and political rights included these items:

- The right to a useful and remunerative job in the industries or shops or farms or mines of the Nation.
- The right to earn enough to provide adequate food and clothing and recreation.
- The right of every farmer to raise and sell his products at a return which will give him and his family a decent living.
- The right of every businessman, large and small, to trade in an atmosphere of freedom from unfair competition and domination by monopolies at home or abroad.

[8]Two important accounts of Roosevelt's assault on fear are Ira Katznelson, *Fear Itself: The New Deal and the Origins of Our Time* (New York: W. W. Norton, 2013) and Michele Landis Dauber, *The Sympathetic State: Disaster Relief and the Origins of the American Welfare State* (Chicago: University of Chicago Press, 2013).

- The right of every family to a decent home.
- The right to adequate medical care and the opportunity to achieve and enjoy good health.
- The right to adequate protection from the economic fears of old age, sickness, accident, and unemployment.

The New Deal comes in for a lot of bashing today, since many people vaguely think of it as a left-wing movement motivated by envy of elites. But those people have forgotten what the Depression was like and how the simple things mentioned here—realized by policies including Federal Deposit Insurance, laws against monopolies, unemployment insurance, Social Security, Medicare, Medicaid, and some type of health policy, whether a revised Affordable Care Act or some suitable alternative—have protected every one of us from the misery of hunger and helplessness. Those things did not exist before Congress enacted them. They may cease to exist in the near future. And yet if we ask what makes the American Dream plausible, what makes a decent level of confidence in one's prospects plausible, we should look here, and then carry on the incomplete work that lies in front of us.

Roosevelt saw that rights protect democracy from envy. What every single person has by right, people can't envy in their fellows. Moving some key economic goods into the rights category undercuts envy, to at least some degree. One reason we see so much envy is that people are not secure in their economic lives. Alexander Hamilton would agree. Far from denouncing elite bankers, as do so many on the left today, he knew that creating a stable economy, including an excellent national bank, was a crucial part of reassuring people, limiting instability, and putting the new nation on a steady course. That doesn't mean that such a system cannot become unjust, and we must always search for the roots of injustice and inequality in our economic system. But it's another matter to hate bankers as such. It's a jolt, but a salutary one, to see young people cheering for the banker, and we should applaud Miranda for, among other things, undercutting the politics of envy by his surprising choice of a hero.

Envy will never disappear. It is deeply rooted in the insecurity of human life itself. Searching for purity, whether in people or in politics, is a recipe for self-hatred and hatred of others. Instead, we can rein in envy by creating conditions in which it will not grow out of hand, conditions in which love and creative work (exemplified by Washington and Hamilton in the musical) set the nation's course. Our nation began (at least mythically) with such a victory. Can we continue in that spirit, or will we soon live, like the ancient Romans, in envy's empire?

6

A TOXIC BREW: SEXISM AND MISOGYNY

No account of our political moment could fail to dwell on the politics of gender. How could any observer fail to notice the remarkable hostility to women that surfaced during the recent campaign? The fact that the US almost elected a female president but didn't was no incidental fact about the election of 2016, whether gender determined the result or not. (Given the narrow result, it's impossible to know this.)

The US is hardly the only nation to face issues of gender bias and hostility. All nations have subordinated women for centuries, and it is likely that none is free today from bias against women in politics—although in nations with a parliamentary system rather than a direct presidential election, women have been rising to top offices with regularity (Indira Gandhi, Golda Meir, Margaret Thatcher, Angela Merkel, Theresa May).

Still, it's something to ponder. Let's start with a list of things our president has said about women, presumably well designed to please his "base":

1. BLOOD. On August 7, 2015, Trump appeared to comment on Megyn Kelly's menstrual period, saying, "You could see there was blood coming out of her eyes. Blood coming out of her wherever."[1] (Trump later said he meant her nose.)

   On June 29, 2017, Trump attacked reporter Mika Brzezinski, saying that on a visit to his Mar-a-Lago club she insisted on joining him, but he "said no!" because she "was bleeding badly from a facelift."[2]

2. WEIGHT. On September 27, 2016, Trump mocked Miss Universe winner Alicia Machado, calling her "Miss Piggy" and "Miss Eating Machine" because she allegedly gained weight after winning.[3] Over the years he has attacked comedian Rosie O'Donnell as "disgusting," and as a "slob" and "pig."[4,5]

3. BATHROOM. On December 21, 2015, Trump commented on Hillary Clinton's bathroom break: "I know where she

[1]https://www.washingtonpost.com/news/post-politics/wp/2015/08/07/trump-says-foxs-megyn-kelly-had-blood-coming-out-of-her-wherever/?utm_term=.e9badd71dab7.

[2]http://money.cnn.com/2017/06/29/media/mika-brzezinski-donald-trump-tweet/index.html.

[3]https://www.washingtonpost.com/news/the-fix/wp/2016/09/27/alicia-machado-the-woman-trump-called-miss-housekeeping-is-ready-to-vote-against-donald-trump/?utm_term=.96bb895b92cb.

[4]http://www.businessinsider.com/trump-rosie-odonnell-history-2017-5/?r=AU&IR=T

[5]https://www.washingtonpost.com/news/post-politics/wp/2015/12/21/donald-trump-calls-hillary-clinton-disgusting-for-using-the-restroom-during-a-debate/?utm_term=.dfae51490c16.

went—it's disgusting. I don't want to talk about it. No, it's too disgusting."

4. BREASTFEEDING. In 2011, when attorney Elizabeth Beck requested a break from a deposition to pump breast milk, "He got up, his face got red, he shook his finger at me, and he screamed, 'You're disgusting, you're disgusting,' and he ran out of there." (Beck recalled the incident in an interview on CNN on July 29, 2015.)[6]
5. ATTRACTIVENESS. On October 28, 2012, Trump called Bette Midler "an extremely unattractive woman."[7] On August 28, 2012, he called Ariana Huffington "unattractive both inside and out."[8] When women came forward by October 13, 2016, to accuse him of inappropriate sexual behavior, following the release of a video in which he boasts of such conduct, Trump insulted one accuser, saying, "Look at her . . . I don't think so."[9]

In September 2015, during an earlier phase of the campaign, he mocked candidate Carly Fiorina's face with a facial expression of disgust, saying: "*Look* at that face! Would anyone *vote* for that? Can you imagine that, the face of our next *president*? . . . I mean, she's a woman, and I'm not

[6]http://edition.cnn.com/2015/07/29/politics/trump-breast-pump-statement/index.html.

[7]http://edition.cnn.com/2017/06/29/politics/kfile-trump-long-history-disparaging-comments/index.html.

[8]Ibid. The story contains numerous other similar examples.

[9]https://www.washingtonpost.com/video/politics/trump-responds-to-allegations-from-reporter-look-at-her-look-at-her-words/2016/10/13/0e266b8a-9175-11e6-bc00-1a9756d4111b_video.html?utm_term=.65d2877360ae.

s'posedta say bad things, but really, folks, come on. Are we *serious*?"[10]

In 2011, Gail Collins wrote a column making fun of Trump's claims of vast wealth. He mailed her a copy of her own column with her picture circled and "Face of a Dog" written over it.[11]

In October 2016, he commented on Hillary Clinton's rear-view appearance, as she walked out on stage for the start of the presidential debate: "I'm standing at my podium and she walks in front of me, right. She walks in front of me. And when she walked in front of me—believe me, I wasn't impressed."[12]

Such incidents might simply illustrate the idiosyncrasies of Donald Trump were they not made on the campaign trail, to great applause. I am far less interested in Trump's likely views than about what the enthusiasm for these utterances in Trump's "base"—and the fact that they were not disqualifying for the larger group of Americans who voted for him—shows us about attitudes to women in our country. The president's preoccupations are evidently those of a large segment of Americans (mostly but not entirely male). To such disgust-laden attacks, we can add other odd features of the hostility

[10]http://money.cnn.com/2015/09/09/media/donald-trump-rolling-stone-carly-fiorina/index.html.

[11]http://www.nytimes.com/2011/04/02/opinion/02collins.html.

[12]http://edition.cnn.com/2016/10/14/politics/donald-trump-hillary-clinton-appearance-debate/index.html.

displayed to Hillary Clinton throughout the campaign: the repeated rumors and speculations about her health, the grotesque "Pizza-Gate" rumor that Clinton ran a child prostitution ring through a DC pizza parlor, and of course the omnipresent undercurrent of speculation about whether Clinton was really up to the job.

All this seems pretty nasty, but it really doesn't sound like fear. Nonetheless, I'll argue that hostility to women, when they attempt to assume leadership roles, does have roots in fear—but in three different ways, connected to three different emotions we've already investigated. Some hostility is driven by the dynamics of fear-blame: women have gotten out of hand, taking things that are *ours* and refusing to play the helpmeet role that is their proper role. So, they have to be disciplined, put back in "their place." Some hostility is driven by fear-disgust: anxiety about bodily fluids, birth, and corporeality in general lead (some) men to vilify (some) women as "disgusting." Finally, and we see this less in these particular examples than in others we'll get to later, a lot of hostility is driven by fear-envy: women are enjoying unparalleled success in American life, more or less taking over in university and professional school admissions and subsequent employment opportunities, leaving many men (and their families) feeling marginalized and put down, cut off from the good things of life.

As we'll see, these three dynamics are all compatible with one another: we don't have to choose. All three are occurring, and they reinforce one another. And the three dynamics correspond roughly to three different accounts of "the heart of the matter," or the deeper issues at stake, driving opposition to women's full equality, especially in public life. Let's call the first story the story of *the delinquent helpmeet*. What men most of all want from women, this story says, is faithful service and selfless sympathy. While he is a breadwinner, she is a home-maker. She raises children and tends to the home while he goes out into the world. Her generosity and selflessness make his fraught life calmer and gentler. But look: many women don't want to serve any longer. They want their own careers, even in politics! And they have the temerity to ask men to help with housework and child rearing. This violates a primal natural contract. No wonder men are increasingly unhappy, that their longevity and health are declining. Women must be shown that their desertion of duty has consequences. (A minority of men, admittedly, welcome the female breadwinner, feeling liberated from provider anxiety.)

The second story is the story of *woman as embodiment*. In connection with the time-honored human desire to transcend the merely animal, women have frequently been cast as more bodily than men. Because women give birth, because they menstruate, because they receive men's sexual fluids, and because their "nature" seems to be connected to birth and sex, anxiety about embodiment and mortality gets projected onto women. They are dirt, fluid, and death. It is because of this symbolic link with feared aspects of the male self that women must be relegated to the home and closely watched. It is for this reason that their bodily functions must be anxiously policed.

Obviously, these are different stories of the "heart of the matter," but both can be true, and they can act to reinforce one another, upping the ante when women's sexuality is policed and women are urged to confine themselves to the home. Paternity anxiety partakes of both "causes," as we'll see.

And then there is another story, a new "cause" in our own time, although its signs have been around for a long time. This is the story of *women as successful competitors*. Anxiety about competitive success is a very old story in human life, and very general. But it does have its distinctive gendered side. If males grow up defining success in terms of competitive achievement—money, status, admiration, jobs that signify all three—how bad it is to find that, instead of all those men you have to get ahead of, you now have a double competition, since women are flooding in everywhere and doing extremely well, maybe even better than men. This "story" seems to be less uniquely about gender; the same dynamic plays a role in hostility to immigrants. But it is often given a gendered edge by being combined with one of the other "stories": why don't they stay home and take care of us, as nature ordains? Why must they bring their fleshy loose bodies, their breast pumps, their menstrual periods, into our workplaces? For many men, too, the family gives this "story" deep roots: the precocious verbal development of a sister, the felt superiority of a mother. And maybe womb envy is in there somewhere: she has good things I can't have. I am excluded from that zone of happy fertility.

SEXISM AND "MISOGYNY"

Before we go further, a distinction must be explored. People talk about *sexism*, and they also talk about *misogyny*, often using the two words interchangeably. But they are really not interchangeable. At any rate, there are two very different phenomena that we should distinguish, although perhaps the two words do not map perfectly onto the two phenomena. Here I've learned from philosopher Kate Manne's new book, *Down Girl: The Logic of Misogyny*, although I won't be agreeing with her account in all respects.[13]

Sexism, in Manne's useful account, is a set of beliefs. The sexist believes that women are inferior to men, less fit for a variety of important functions. Or, perhaps, the sexist might believe that "nature" dictates that men are fit for employment and political roles, women for domestic roles.

Sexism is amply evident in American history (as in the history of every nation). A typical and famous example of the "two natures" story is Justice Joseph Bradley's opinion in *Bradwell v. Illinois* (83 US 130 (1873)), the Supreme Court case that upheld an Illinois law forbidding women to practice law in Illinois:

> The natural and proper timidity and delicacy which belongs to the female sex evidently unfits it for many of the

[13]New York: Oxford University Press, 2016. My primary disagreement with Manne is that she focuses more or less exclusively on the "bad helpmeet" scenario, mentioning disgust briefly and envy not at all.

> occupations of civil life. The constitution of the family organization, which is founded in the divine ordinance, as well as in the nature of things, indicates the domestic sphere as that which properly belongs to the domain and functions of womanhood. The harmony, not to say identity, of interests and views which belong, or should belong, to the family institution is repugnant to the idea of a woman adopting a distinct and independent career from that of her husband.

Justice Bradley's assertion of female incompetence encounters an immediate obstacle: Myra Bradwell had already been practicing law successfully for a number of years. As editor of the *Chicago Legal News*, she crusaded tirelessly for higher standards in the profession and an upgrading of legal education; in 1873, she became one of the founders of the Chicago Bar Association, which, of course, she was unable to join. Moreover, Iowa admitted a woman to the bar in 1869, and in 1870, a woman had graduated from an Illinois law school (the forerunner of Northwestern University's Pritzker School of Law). Ohio admitted a woman to the bar in 1873. But Justice Bradley was ready:

> It is true that many women are unmarried and not affected by any of the duties, complications, and incapacities arising out of the married state, but these are exceptions to the general rule. The paramount destiny and mission of woman are to fulfil the noble and benign offices of wife and mother.

> This is the law of the Creator. And the rules of civil society must be adapted to the general constitution of things, and cannot be based upon exceptional cases.

There is a glaring problem in this "argument": Myra Bradwell was married.

Sexism, however, often has little interest in data. Indeed, it has a very peculiar illogic, already observed by the great John Stuart Mill in his treatise *The Subjection of Women*, published in 1869. Mill, who introduced the first British bill for women's suffrage as a member of Parliament in 1872,[14] pointed out that sexists must lack confidence in their own judgments of incapacity, since they work so hard to stop women from doing things that, by their own account, women are unable to do: "The anxiety of mankind to interfere in behalf of nature, for fear lest nature should not succeed in effecting its purpose, is an altogether unnecessary solicitude. What women by nature cannot do, it is quite superfluous to forbid them from doing." Indeed, Mill continues, if we examine all the prohibitions and requirements society has organized, we would rationally conclude that men do not believe that "the natural vocation of a woman is that of a wife and mother." Rather, it seems that they must believe that this vocation is not attractive to women: "that if they are free to do anything else—if any other means

[14]The bill failed, of course. Britain got full female suffrage only in 1928 (the US, in 1920). Aaron Burr, of all people, introduced a bill for female suffrage in the New York State legislature in the late 1790s. Burr, a serious feminist, kept a portrait of Mary Wollstonecraft on his study wall. His daughter, Theodosia, was one of the best-educated women of her day.

of living, or occupation of their time and faculties, is open . . . there will not be enough of them who will be willing to accept the condition said to be natural to them."[15]

So, sexism is an uneasy set of beliefs, fraught with hidden uncertainty. The same beliefs, coupled with the same undercurrent of uncertainty, persisted in the US until very recently. Nancy Weiss Malkiel's excellent study of coeducation struggles in the Ivy League, "*Keep the Damned Women Out*": *The Struggle for Coeducation*, offers scores of examples.[16] She focuses on elite institutions, and on WASP culture, but the attitudes she finds there are broadly American, even if Ivy Leaguers have them in an exaggerated form. (Let's not make the mistake of thinking that misogyny is primarily a working-class phenomenon!)

As late as the 1960s and 1970s, lots of leading administrators, faculty members, trustees, and even students of all-male institutions (the account focuses on Yale and Princeton, and the *sui generis* case of Harvard/Radcliffe[17]) were ready to say with no uncertainty that women can't learn as well as men, that they don't belong in institutions that train "leaders" of the country, and that their primary function is that of wife and mother. "Oh, save us from the giggling crowds, the domestic lecture,

[15]J. S. Mill, *The Subjection of Women*, ed. Susan Moller Okin (Indianapolis: Hackett Publishing, 1988), ch. 1.

[16]Princeton: Princeton University Press, 2016. Page numbers are given inside the text.

[17]*Sui generis* because Radcliffe admitted women who (after a brief period of separate classes) took classes with Harvard men and even received Harvard degrees, and yet the illusion of an independent Radcliffe held in place a mandatory admissions quota.

and the home economics classes of a female infiltration," wrote the *Yale Daily News* in 1956 (56). A leading Princeton administrator opined that Princeton was just "too intellectual" for women, who should be trained to become "a good wife, mother, and family person [rather] than a whiz kid" (112).

Women were not the only people excluded by these institutions: racial minorities and Jews were also virtually nonexistent at Yale and Princeton. A new Yale dean of admissions undertook both to advocate coeducation and to broaden the group of men admitted, meeting the usual "leadership" argument by saying that times are changing and leaders are coming from many different groups, including Jews, minorities, women, and public school graduates. He was met, in 1966, with this remarkable riposte from one Trustee:

> His interlocutor shot back, "You're talking about Jews and public school graduates as leaders. Look around you at this table"—he waved a hand at Brewster, [John] Lindsay, [Paul] Moore, Bill Bundy, . . . "These are America's leaders. There are no Jews here. There are no public school graduates here."

Did the speaker have so little self-knowledge that he truly believed that "natural" merit and leadership ability had produced the all-white, male, Protestant, preppy board of trustees? Or was he defiantly announcing his determination to keep the "club" the way it was, excluding outsiders?

This question helps us segue from sexism to "misogyny." This word etymologically means "hatred of women," but its current use is broader. As Manne defines it, for example, it is an enforcement mechanism, a set of behaviors designed to keep women in their place. The trustee would have been preaching sexism, if he argued that women (and Jews and minorities) all lacked the ability to compete at Yale. But it is easier to read his remarks as expressing a determination to enforce privilege: we are at this table, and we won't cede "our" place to any new group. Let's, then, think of *misogyny* as a determined enforcement of gender privilege, which can sometimes be motivated by hatred but is more often combined with benign paternalistic sentiments. Its primary root is self-interest, combined with anxiety about potential loss. (So, it's not symmetrical to female hatred of men, to the extent that this exists: that's anger driven by grievances and a wish for retribution.)

Misogyny is often "justified" by sexism: the reason to deny women university entrance, political offices, etc., is that their "nature" fits them for the role of wife and mother. But sexism is hard to defend with evidence. As Mill points out, the lack of other options for women makes it impossible to know what they are really able to do, and whether they really seek the role of wife and mother. And the fact that they can only be kept in that role by strenuous prohibitions suggests that they are actually eager to have a wider range of choices. So, misogyny often waves a sexist banner but is basically all about the defense of entrenched privilege: *we like things this way, and we won't let them change.*

Which attitude do Trump's remarks suggest? On the whole, sexism is hard to illustrate, since his remarks about female incompetence focus on the specific case of Hillary Clinton. More often, he seems to be delivering what we might call a "smackdown" to women who achieve in formerly all-male jobs (and who have the audacity to challenge him on some issue), by jeers, insults, manifestations of disgust. He doesn't say that a breastfeeding or menstruating woman can't be a good lawyer or journalist, he just tries to make life in those professions difficult for such women by public humiliation. So, the misogyny label fits him, and his audience too, better than the sexism label.

This may be the place to remark that, although this chapter focuses criticism on Trump supporters, misogyny also has a long history on the American left. The radical movements of the 1960s and 1970s, prominently including SDS (Students for a Democratic Society) and SNCC (Student Nonviolent Coordinating Committee), excluded women from leadership positions and failed to listen to their demands for a rethinking of domestic responsibilities. As Malkiel insists, they were in that respect as bad as the Yale-Princeton old guard (18–19). Women had to make our own movement, although today that movement gets a great deal of support from men.

Let's return to Justice Bradley. At first reading, he appears to be a sexist, but on closer inspection his primary attitude is one of misogyny. After talking about natural destinies, etc., he gets around to the real point: we can admit that some unmarried women seek to practice law, but we won't allow married women to do so. Nor does he say that a married woman is *unable* to practice law. He says that these women have other "duties" that they should be required to do, some of which (raising children, mainly) are "incapacities" when it comes to practicing law. Very similar to Justice Bradley, in our own time, is Pastor Ralph Drollinger, the evangelical leader who offers Bible study sessions for members of President Trump's cabinet. Drollinger writes that women with children who serve in legislatures far from their home are "sinners." Like Justice Bradley, he says not that they are incompetent, but that they are breaking a rule.[18]

Similarly, the conservatives at Yale and Princeton who struggled against coeducation used sexist arguments, but those arguments were flimsy by that time, given that most universities in the nation had long been coed, and women were doing very well there. Their real concern was the one the trustee expressed: keeping the leadership "club" male (and white and Christian). Sexism says, "Poor women, they will always underperform." Misogyny says, "Keep the damned women out."

The tension between sexism and misogyny is great, as Mill says. If women are really weak and not up to performing in a given area, things will sort themselves out in the market. So, if we see energetic efforts to erect barricades, this suggests that the defenders really don't think that things will sort themselves out. The history of coeducation in US universities shows this tension clearly: for it is typically when women perform really well, taking more than "their share" of the spaces in a class, that the desire to keep them out waxes strong. My own university, coed at its inception in 1892, rapidly grew to a majority of women on a merit-based admissions policy, and between 1892 and 1902 women accounted for more than 56 percent

[18]http://www.latimes.com/politics/la-na-la-pol-trump-cabinet-pastor-20170803-story.html.

of elections to Phi Beta Kappa, the academic honor society. At that point President William Rainey Harper created a side track for women, with separate classes in introductory courses. What he said was that alumni giving would fall off. But fear for the future of the "club" was palpable.

To the credit of the institution, Harper's experiment was short-lived. Never fully implemented, it ceased at his death in 1906. Not so short-lived was the reluctance of Harvard, Yale, and Princeton to use equal-access admissions. For a long time, the ratio of males to females in the Harvard entering class was held artificially at four to one, using the fiction of a separate Radcliffe (which had never had a faculty of its own). Similarly, Yale tried admitting 250 women and 1,000 men in the first few classes, so that no male student would feel "his place" compromised. As Malkiel points out, the first Yale women, admitted on straight grades and test scores, typically outperformed the men, admitted on all sorts of criteria, including alumni connections, athletic accomplishments, and the more nebulous trait of being "promising."

Misogyny, as I'm defining it here, is a determination to protect entrenched interests. It may use sexist beliefs as a tool, but the tool sometimes turns into a double-edged sword, so the misogynist typically won't rely on it too much. (Thus, in the parallel case of anti-Semitism, people rarely tried to say that Jews could not do the intellectual work of lawyers in "white-shoe" firms, or could not do the work at Yale. They would substitute some other "argument," such as the common claim that Jews were vulgar and socially obnoxious, a claim virtually impossible to falsify.[19]) Similarly, someone can be determined to keep (most) women in the roles of wife, mother, and sex object without really believing in female inferiority.

Indeed, it seems that our friend Rousseau, enigmatic and contradictory as always, is much more a misogynist than a sexist. In Book V of *Emile*, his great book on education, he gives the surface appearance of portraying Sophie, Emile's destined spouse, as inclined by nature to please and support men. But when you read the text with care, you see that at every point Rousseau allows his reader to observe that Sophie's strong natural inclinations in the direction of physical and intellectual achievement have been forcibly curbed. She isn't allowed to read the same books, she has to run a race in high-heeled shoes (and almost beats Emile anyway).[20] The real driving force in the text is the thought that social stability and order require confining women to a domestic role. In a telling footnote, Rousseau says that in some societies women can have a couple of children and still have employment outside the home. But in Europe, with its disease-ridden cities, people have to have at least four children to ensure that two survive, and that means

[19]See my "Jewish Men, Jewish Lawyers: Roth's 'Eli, the Fanatic' and the Question of Jewish Masculinity in American Law," in Saul Levmore and Martha C. Nussbaum, eds., *American Guy: Masculinity in American Law and Literature* (New York: Oxford University Press, 2014), 165–201.

[20]This understanding of the text is convincingly argued by Susan Moller Okin in her *Women in Western Political Thought* (Princeton: Princeton University Press, 1979, new edition with introduction by Debra Satz, 2013), part III.

that the woman has to become a full-time mother.[21] That's an argument for enforced domesticity. It isn't really sexism.

FEAR-BLAME

Let's now start to sort out the different strands in misogyny, asking what this desire to keep women in "their place" is all about. One strand in misogyny (the one on which Manne's book focuses) is a male wish to have women available to support their needs and to dedicate their lives to them. Part of this may be about sexual service, part about child care. But let's start with the bare idea that giving to men is what women are *for*. Consider Shel Silverstein's poem *The Giving Tree*, which used to be read to young children as a touching nice story about mother and child.[22] This poem is about a tree (characterized as female) who loves a little boy. The boy relies on the tree for play, food, and sleep. Both are happy. As the boy grows older, he asks the tree for money, and then a house for his wife and children: and the tree gives him her branches to carry away to build a house. He stays away for a long time, and then returns, this time asking for a boat. The tree gives him her trunk, and he cuts it down and builds a boat and sails away. Finally, the boy comes back again, and the tree apologizes: she has nothing left to give him. Her trunk, her branches, and her apples have all been given away. She is just a stump. The boy says he wants to sit and rest, so the tree says

[21]Bloom edition, 362.

[22]Shel Silverstein, *The Giving Tree* (New York: Harper and Row, 1964). Manne discusses the poem well.

that an old stump is nice for sitting and resting. The boy sits. "And the tree was happy."

This alarming narrative seems totally out of place in the education of children, and yet it once flourished there.[23] The "tree," or mother, gives and gives and gives, until she is just a stump. And the boy is never interested in giving anything back, he just uses the tree in different ways. But somehow this is the way things are supposed to be, and the tree is happy because the boy still wants to use her. (There are other themes in the poem, about aging and loss; but the gender dynamics make it impossible to focus on these more humanly interesting aspects.) The nuclear family in many eras, and certainly in the 1950s, just before protest broke out, was romanticized and gendered in just this way. The toll the life of service took on women was vaguely acknowledged but somehow thought to make for her happiness. Men felt that they could not go out into the world, adventure, and achieve, unless they could rely on that tree being always there at home to come back to.

The romance of women as givers has several different aspects. Some versions of the story focus on homemaking and domesticity, some on child-bearing and child-rearing. Some (though not Silverstein's) focus on the woman's availability for sex and her duty to keep herself attractive so that the man will have a nice sex partner to come home to.

To that rather bourgeois point about sex, our friend Rousseau adds three others: (1) men won't want to raise children

[23]My research assistant Nethanel Lipshitz, from Israel, read the book in Hebrew translation and was totally unaware that the tree was female: in Hebrew both boy and tree are male.

unless the confinement of women to the home assures them that the children are really theirs; (2) male passion may flag if it is not constantly kindled by female "coyness," which women will cunningly deploy as fiancées and then as wives; (3) on the other hand, male passion might become distracting and overwhelming, unless women keep it under control by insisting that men confine sexuality to marriage, which will predictably cause desire to decline. As you can see, Rousseau is on many sides of this issue, but always with insight. All three points may be true of some people, though it is difficult to imagine a single person—perhaps excepting Rousseau himself—of whom all three would be true at roughly the same time.[24] Thomas Jefferson follows Rousseau, repeating his first and third arguments: "Were our state a pure democracy . . . there would yet be excluded from [our] deliberations . . . women, who, to prevent depravation of morals, and ambiguity of issue, could not mix promiscuously in the public meetings of men."[25]

The story of "woman as giving tree" is often freighted with anxiety—not least in our time. Consider the boy in the story. Now he's all grown up, and he wants to bring up children. But women aren't playing by the rules any longer. They don't stay at home, they get jobs, they earn incomes, and they ask that grown-up boy to share housework and child care. This is not

[24]The first and third views are stated in *Emile*; the third is implied there but is explicit in the *Letter to d'Alembert*.

[25]Jefferson, letter to Samuel Kercheval, September 5, 1816; Jefferson also excludes "infants" and slaves. This sentence is often quoted incorrectly, saying "ambiguity of issues" instead of "issue" (offspring).

what life prepared me for, he thinks. It's unfair. I want things to be as they were. Maybe he also has a female boss. He sees women running for political office. Again, he thinks, *It's just not fair. They should be supporting me, but instead they are demanding and giving orders.* Not raised for reciprocal love, he expects service, and lo and behold, it isn't there.

This boy might well fall back on sexism, saying women's natural place is in the home. But the real issue is misogyny: get back there where you belong. A deep anxiety gets blended with rage: they are the ones who have made my life so insecure.

Sometimes the fear-blame reaction targets all women. More often, though, it exempts docile and traditional women who play the old game pretty well. (And, of course, there are women who want to play that game: being taken care of by a breadwinner is, to some, appealing.) Fear and blame (including blame from those more conventional women) target those "uppity" ones who want to change the game. Hence Kate Manne's title, *Down Girl*. To the nice little doggie, you don't need to say "down." You say that to an obstreperous dog, who hasn't learned how to behave.

Here we see one reason so many women voted for Donald Trump. There are, of course, many reasons. Many women simply agreed with Trump's positions on other issues and decided to disregard his comments about women. But some, at least, object on moral or religious grounds to women who pursue personal independence and career success, rather than making care for home and family their primary concern. They blame the "rule breakers" for their alleged selfishness—and sometimes that blame is further fueled by a sense that they themselves, by putting traditional duties first, may have missed something.

Such complaints raise a genuinely difficult issue. Many children in our society do get too little parental care and time. This problem, however, is most often caused by poverty, which necessitates long hours of work and makes quality child care unavailable. It is also compounded by high rates of incarceration, which rob many poor families of a male parent. So, our problems of child neglect are not very closely connected to the alleged problem of "uppity" women. But even in those cases where selfishness is part of the problem, surely blame for irresponsibility should not be put entirely on women: what about men, who still don't share fairly in care and domestic labor? And what about workplaces, which still do not sufficiently accommodate the lives of two-income families? While we should honor any spouse, male or female, who chooses to stay at home and care for children (and sometimes aging parents), the traditional model, which gave men free choice and told women that they had no choice, is surely wrong in a society of equals.

The "Down, girl" response, in short, deflects attention from the real social problems that need to be solved: problems of poverty, problems of mass incarceration, problems of workplace inflexibility, and problems of genuine choice and equality.

FEAR-ENVY

Sexism was comforting to the anxious misogynist: they can't do as well as we can anyway. As soon as a group manifests superior achievement, that prop falls away, and fear escalates. Anti-Semitism never really had a prop, since the superior achievements of Jews were well known, so a fake prop was invented in the form of slurs about Jewish behavior and culture. What about women? Already in the era covered by Malkiel's book, people could see that women were outperforming men in many universities, and that they would claim "too many" slots if admitted on a basis of equality.

Today the story of higher education is ever more alarming to men who feel that certain slots are "theirs" by right. Women are outperforming men as applicants virtually everywhere. Indeed, a common story I hear from schools that are strongly attached to their male athletic programs is that those schools artificially hold down the number of women so that they won't be required by Title IX to cut expenditures on male sports. (Title IX requires that the proportion of expenditure on male and female sports correspond to the proportions of men and women in the student body.) One football school told me that the ratio of women to men dictated by grades and scores would be at least 60 to 40, maybe higher. But they hold it to 55 (women)/45 (men) for the sake of the football program. Other schools skew the ratio artificially in order to produce a balanced social atmosphere, reasoning that both men and women will reject a school whose sex ratio is too skewed. (Sarah Lawrence, which does not skew, is 71 percent female.[26])

The story of women's achievements is international. In countries that depend more on test scores than we do, and

[26]https://www.sarahlawrence.edu/about/.

less on alumni connections, athletics, or hobbies, women are eclipsing men virtually everywhere. For example, although Americans have a stereotype of the Arab world as hostile to women's achievements, women outnumbered men as university students in 2012 in Algeria, Bahrain, Kuwait, Lebanon, Morocco, Tunisia, Qatar, Oman, Syria, Saudi Arabia, and the United Arab Emirates.[27] In Jordan, women not only lead men by 52 percent to 48 percent, they really clean up at the top university, the University of Jordan in Amman, where I was told on a visit in 2007 that women comprise 75 percent of the student body. Women still face severe employment barriers in all these countries, but how long can they be kept out of the leadership "club" when their achievements in tertiary education are so impressive?

When women succeed, what happens to men? The story of Harvard, Princeton, and Yale offers a microcosm of a question that looms large in our nation as a whole (especially given the changing requirements of the economy, which make a college degree a must for most jobs). For a while, the leaders of these Ivy League institutions tried to pretend that there was no zero-sum competition: places for women would simply be added, but the number of men would remain constant. That strategy didn't work over the long haul, of course. None of these

[27]http://edition.cnn.com/2012/06/01/world/meast/middle-east-women-education/index.html. The data were compiled by the UN. See also http://monitor.icef.com/2014/07/increasing-participation-by-women-in-middle-east-education/ and the more comprehensive data in http://monitor.icef.com/2014/10/women-increasingly-outpacing-mens-higher-education-participation-many-world-markets/.

institutions ever contemplated simply doubling the number of places they offered, a financially and logistically unworkable idea, since it would have meant doubling residences, greatly increasing faculty size, etc. As pressure rose to admit a more nearly equal number of women, and as admissions decisions gradually heeded qualifications rather than aiming for a rigid quota for women, the number of men sooner or later had to decline. The three institutions resisted equal access for a long time. At Harvard, the fiction of Radcliffe's autonomy served to hold the four-to-one admissions quota in place through the 1970s, and the two colleges merged fully only in 1999.

Surprisingly, the fact that there are surely fewer places for men than formerly at Harvard, Yale, and Princeton has not created much of a backlash these days. Rich alumni have daughters as well as sons; alumnae gradually filtered into the ranks of donors; some expansion of class sizes lessened the shock of diminished access. But above all, people became convinced that coeducation was essential to attract the best students, and worries about how it would work in practice gradually waned.

In American society as a whole, there is no such happy ending. Even though people sort of believe that all people's talents should be developed and that everyone has a right to compete in education, employment, and the political arena, the unavoidable fact is that doubling the applicant pool, in all these areas, means many disappointments for many men. It also means other changes for which American men of my generation were not at all prepared: above all, more men doing more housework, child care, and elder care. As I've mentioned, the left-wing movements of my generation were very male-dominated, and had no interest in the equal division of domestic work. This issue was raised mainly by women, and it is still an exceedingly difficult one in families all over the country—especially given that our country, unlike many, does not subsidize child care for preschool children or even universal pre-K education, and has a comparatively weak family and medical leave program.

Envy flares up, I said, when a group feels cut out of key good things that other people have (money, status, offices, employment opportunities). There's no doubt that white men, particularly in the lower middle classes, are indeed losing out. The jobs that are available mostly require a college degree. Even men who are employed face income stagnation and declining purchasing power. The glaring health problems in this group, opiate addiction above all, are signs of misery and hopelessness. Nobel Prize–winning economist Angus Deaton and his wife and co-author Anne Case see a "sea of despair" among non-Hispanic white working-class men.[28] Mortality has skyrocketed in both sexes, for those with no college degree, but is higher among males. They attribute the rise to bad employment prospects and to the cumulative disadvantage of obesity, drug use, and stress, as behaviors initially sought to treat disappointment make prospects worse.

What interests me is the interaction between the stress and anxiety produced by bad prospects and a type of despairing envy that lashes out against those who are seen as displacing them.

[28]A good summary of their work is at https://www.washingtonpost.com/national/health-science/new-research-identifies-a-sea-of-despair-among-white-working-class-americans/2017/03/22/c777ab6e-0da6-11e7-9b0d-d27c98455440_story.html?utm_term=.8e053e1e6b88.

This particular envy dynamic requires a belief in one's own privileged entitlement: "they" have taken "our" place. Immigrants bear the brunt of some of this envy, but women get a very large share—easy to understand, given the sudden ascent of women in all aspects of American life. Disparate educational success is particularly relevant, since many women escape, to some extent, the employment problems of men of similar background. At any rate, seeing the prominence of women in education and jobs requiring education, it's easy to blame them for men's problems.

One small yet telling example of envy-driven misogyny was a crisis over a website called AutoAdmit that purported to offer advice about law school admissions. The site quickly degenerated, however, becoming a mainly pornographic site on which anonymous male law students told fictional obscene stories about named female law students. Even if employers didn't believe the formulaic porn stories, they had a tainting effect, and women felt that it did real harm in their job searches—besides producing stress in the classroom, since the defamers clearly knew the women personally, and yet the women could not trace their defamers' identity. When two women—high-achieving Yale Law School students—sued for defamation, they were only able to identify some of the posters. They eventually settled with some of those involved; the terms of the lawsuit, however, remain confidential. The law school community took this very seriously, and it was a central exhibit in a 2008 conference about Internet law that later became an edited collection.[29]

[29]Saul Levmore and Martha C. Nussbaum, eds., *The Offensive Internet: Speech, Privacy, and Reputation* (Cambridge, MA: Harvard University Press, 2010).

My own contribution discussed connections between the sentiments expressed on the site and philosopher Friedrich Nietzsche's idea of *ressentiment*. *Ressentiment*, for Nietzsche, is an envious emotion felt by the powerless toward the powerful, but then it becomes creative: it prompts the powerless to invent an alternative universe in which they are powerful and their competitors are pathetic. That, I said, was what Internet porn makes possible: an alternative universe in which the woman is not a successful achiever, but simply a slut; and this universe has effects in the real world. Fortunately, this sort of bullying, still common elsewhere on the Internet, is not typical in today's law schools, where women are achieving ever greater parity.

This is what I now see happening more generally with American misogyny. In reality, women are achieving ever more success. In the alternative universe of the misogynist (the people who cheered at Trump's remarks), women are pathetic, disgusting, sluttish, weak, ugly. In the real world more and more women are refusing to play the role of charming helper. They insist on other criteria of success. In the parallel universe of misogyny, those who don't play that role are jeered at as abysmal failures. Unfortunately, misogyny in America at large is far more influential than it is in law schools.

The fear-envy-misogyny story fits well with the fear-blame story: men feel bested by women in a zero-sum competition and at the very same time they also fail to find the unequivocal support and undemanding comfort that women once offered as "homemakers." Or if they do find it in their own homes, they know well that the institution of the "giving tree" is rapidly dying out.

FEAR-DISGUST

Trump's remarks, however, appeal above all to disgust. Sometimes they target women who don't fit a narrow male norm of attractiveness: women who are overweight or aging. But many of his remarks evince a more general disgust at women's bodily fluids: breast milk, menstrual blood, blood from a face-lift (where he would have seen no blood surely, only bruising and possibly stitches), the imagined urine or feces of Hillary Clinton's bathroom trip. And his audience goes along with all these references, finding it delightful that women (including conventionally attractive women) are characterized as zones of disgusting liquid. Why?

Misogynistic disgust has a long history and has been much studied. For some strange reason (given that all human beings excrete and bleed) women have often been cast by men as somehow more bodily, more animal, more bound up with stench and decay, than men. Is it because women give birth and are thus associated indelibly with vulnerable embodiment? Or, as legal theorist William Ian Miller suggests, is it the fact that men leave their own fluids behind in the woman and therefore think of her as a receptacle of the sticky stuff they discharge?[30] (This would fit with the way in which disgust toward gay men focuses obsessively on anal intercourse.) Who knows. These things are hardly logical. What is clear is that many whole cultures have seen women as somehow more bodily, more animal,

[30]William Ian Miller, *The Anatomy of Disgust* (Cambridge, MA: Harvard University Press, 1997).

than men, and have seen men as capable of transcending their mere humanity only on condition that they keep women confined and keep their bodily functions under close control. Taboos surrounding menstruation, birth, and sex are ubiquitous. And that's a type of misogyny, if we mean what I mean by that word, the enforcement of a lower status for women.

Obviously that sort of misogyny is compatible with sexual desire. Often disgust follows gratified desire. As Adam Smith remarks of male desire, "When we have dined, we order the covers to be removed."[31] (Smith, a hypochondriac who lived with his mother until her death shortly before her ninetieth birthday, is not known to have had any sexual experience, so he is probably talking about his culture rather than making a personal remark.) But often the two are more profoundly linked: the woman is alluring for the very reason that she is disgusting: she represents embodiment, which is feared but also coveted. Sigmund Freud believed that for this reason all sexual desire is inevitably mingled with disgust. I'm sure he is wrong, but the fact that he said this shows how widespread the link was, or is.

Disgust-misogyny is clearly fear-driven, like all projective disgust: what is feared is death and mortal embodiment. But if women represent that feared (but often desired) condition, then they represent dirt and death, and are feared, hence disciplined and controlled, for precisely that reason.

[31]Smith, *The Theory of Moral Sentiments*, ed. D. D. Raphael and A. L. Macfie (Indianapolis: Liberty Classics, 1982), I.ii.1.2, 28.

The disgust-misogyny story is a very different story about the "root of the matter" from *The Giving Tree* story or the envy-competition story. It is appealing because it gets at something deep in people that is not simply the creation of a single political moment. But we don't have to choose. The stories are not incompatible; they are complementary and even mutually reinforcing. I'm inclined to say that the disgust story could not explain the outbreak of misogyny we see in America today without the other two stories. Fear and insecurity never go away entirely, and human fears focus insistently on the body and mortality. But fear can be dramatically exacerbated by rapid social changes that appear to remove a source of comfort and undemanding love. And it can be further exacerbated by economic conditions that make competitive envy soar upward, especially when envy has an obvious target: a competitor who used to help you and who now takes your job.

Sexism is a problem. But sexist beliefs can be refuted by evidence. By and large they have been refuted. The real problem is many men's determination to maintain the old order, by any means possible: ridicule, expressions of disgust, refusals to hire, to elect, to respect as equals. Misogyny is not a very intelligent strategy, since it is purely negative: "Keep the Damned Women Out." It's like a child stamping a foot: no, no, no. Refusing change doesn't solve the health problems of working-class men or help all of us extend university education and its opportunities to more of our people, problems that misogynists themselves want to solve. Nor does it solve a problem they have hardly begun to face: how to reinvent love, care, and the nuclear family in an era of increasing female work and achievement. Misogyny is comforting for a moment but achieves nothing.

Once again, what we need is not more of this toxic brew, it is, instead, strategies that move us beyond what we might call the Fear Family, and into cooperative work for a more promising future with one another.

7

HOPE, LOVE, VISION

For the city I make my prayer,
prophesying with kind intent,
that in plenty the blessings
that make life prosperous
may be made to burgeon from the earth
by the sun's radiant beam.

—Aeschylus, *Eumenides*
(English translation by Hugh Lloyd-Jones)

Let us live here in tranquility and our hearts be softened.
Let us build a bridge upon the abyss that's opened up
between us.
Let us love our brother, our friends, for no good reason.
Let a smile shine from their eyes like the sun upon the ocean.

—Danny Maseng (contemporary Israeli American
songwriter), "Sim Shalom"

June 15, 2017. It's a bad day today, after the shooting of Republican congressman Steve Scalise and others at a congressional baseball game, by a disturbed man apparently motivated by hatred of Trump and Republicans. But it seems that more or less every day, these days, is a bad day. Everyone talks about how our society is falling apart, riven by fear, anger, disgust, and envy. Where, then, is hope? How can we have it? How can we propel ourselves into constructive action in this time of fear and rage?

Okay, what grounds for hope do I myself think about, as I examine my recent days in Chicago? The search for hope is always personal, so let me begin with my own, on June 15. I think first of my friends and family, my colleagues, the solid commitment our university community has to the reasoned exchange of differing views, the way we meet so often to differ and to criticize, in an atmosphere of equal respect for young and old, and civil engagement between left and right. I know this is not how academic life goes everywhere in the world. I've just returned from a country where academics have just been told by a government policy paper that they may not even mention their political views in class. I am currently writing an article about another country where students face arbitrary arrest and limitless detention if they assemble for peaceful protest.[1] So: if my own corner of America is still healthy (not without issues, but basically), that counts for something.

I think, too, that so far, the basic institutions of our government are reasonably healthy. Courts are not ideal deliberative bodies, but they aren't corrupt tools of power either, as in some countries, and the separation of powers works well on the whole.

I think about the deeply troubled race relations in my city, with the escalation of gun violence during the past year; but I also think of some good signs, such as the fact that our new police chief seems to have the confidence of both the African American community and the police force, so one can start to hope that reasonable reforms will be implemented over time (although it is hard to know how much they can accomplish without major gun control laws).

But hopes need to feed on particulars, so what concrete events do mine feed on? How do I manage to flip the switch, so to speak, on Thursday, June 15, from dark thoughts of gunfire and social decay to prospects for peace, reconciliation, and progress? It's no accident, I think, that my thoughts reflect my own obsessions about how we pursue peace and progress—through the arts and through respectful argument.

I think of the Concert for Peace held on June 11 at St. Sabina Church on Chicago's South Side by cellist Yo-Yo Ma, in

[1]The first is Israel (where the government's position paper, an "ethical code" for academics, was vigorously contested and has not been implemented); the second is India, where the situation is far more grave, and yet there is also courageous resistance by people defending that nation's long tradition of freedom of expression.

cooperation with the Reverend Michael Pfleger, leading race-relations activist and senior priest of Chicago's largest African American Catholic parish, joined by the majority-minority Chicago Children's Choir, which brought out a large and passionate crowd and raised $70,000 for Pfleger's programs for African American youth.[2] Nobody can rest, Pfleger said, "until peace becomes a reality in the city of Chicago." The lifelong investment of Pfleger and the new commitment of the elite Chicago Symphony Orchestra to the South Side (they arranged Ma's participation, and the concert is part of a series of events in the neighborhoods), give me hope.

I reread a speech given by my former student, first-term US congressman from California Ro Khanna, at the University of Chicago's Class Day on June 9, calling for self-examination, for "quieter voices," for a stepping back from the loud and self-assured style of politics to a more thoughtful style of interaction. "We need thinkers. We need listeners. We need those who have studied history enough to be skeptical about easy slogans or simple promises."[3] That's easy to say, but I know that Ro is bringing these demands and values to his work in Washington. That does give me hope.

I wasn't at St. Sabina, but I too participated around that time in a musical and religious event about peace and reconciliation—at my Reform temple, KAM Isaiah Israel on Chicago's South Side, a temple with a long record of civil rights

[2]http://www.chicagotribune.com/entertainment/music/vonrhein/ct-classical-yo-yo-ma-ent-0614-20170613-column.html.

[3]Text sent me by the author; on file with me.

activism and work on behalf of immigrants and other minorities. Our cantor, David Berger, a gifted musician who has rescued from oblivion a lot of the music of German and French synagogues from the 1920s and 1930s, joined with me to do a Words and Music program about anger and reconciliation, in which I lectured for a while, then he sang, and back and forth for an hour, ending with questions from the audience. Berger, a gay man married to a Conservative rabbi, both adoptive parents of an African American boy, radiates joy and vision, singing material ranging from Yiddish folksongs to a song from Kurt Weill's *Lost in the Stars* (a musical about reconciliation in South Africa) and an extract from Leonard Bernstein's *Mass*, and concluding with the contemporary Danny Maseng song, "Sim Shalom" ("Grant Peace," about reconciliation between Israelis and Palestinians, but also among all people).

Together Berger and I try our best to embody two things that are central to a politics of hope, as I'll articulate it in this chapter: loving, imaginative vision (through poetry, music, and the other arts), and a spirit of deliberation and rational critique, embodied in philosophy, but also in good political discourse everywhere. (This division of roles Is somewhat artificial, since I sing in the temple choir and Berger often gives insightful and philosophical sermons.) And in this case, I don't just think about it, I try to do it. Hope is not and cannot be inert. It requires action, commitment. These events were small and hardly earth-shaking. But we all derive emotional sustenance from small daily things more than from large abstractions. And it seems that this emotional sustenance is crucial if our lives in general are to produce anything that is good and useful. That sustenance was what I was after, as I steered my thoughts, on June 15.

DEFINING HOPE

So what is hope? It is a puzzling emotion. And oddly, despite its importance, it is not often extensively discussed by philosophers. One common view is clearly inadequate: that hope involves a desire for an outcome, combined with an assessment that this outcome is quite likely.[4] This seems wrong for three reasons. First, hope really does not depend on our assessment of probabilities. People hope for a good medical outcome for themselves or their loved ones even when the prognosis is grim. Indeed, as the probability of a good outcome rises, hope starts to seem superfluous and is often replaced by cheerful expectation. (The same thing happens with fear: as the bad outcome gets close to certainty, fear turns to despair or fatalism, or to mind-numbing terror.)

Furthermore, that propensity to hope in dire times seems connected somehow with the eventual good outcome, if one occurs. If the patient or the family abandons hope (or wrongly inflates hope to overconfident expectation), that is likely to mean that new treatments won't be tried. If a nation gives up hope when attacked by a powerful enemy, it won't undertake

[4]The history of such philosophical discussions is well summarized by Adrienne Martin in *How We Hope: A Moral Psychology* (Princeton: Princeton University Press, 2013). My arguments against the "received view" are similar to hers.

courageous strategies that may ultimately prove successful. The connection between hope and action is important, as we'll see.

The second problem with the desire-probability view is that hope involves not just a desire for something good, but an evaluation of it as importantly good, worth pursuing. (This evaluation might be mistaken, so we're just talking about what the person thinks.) I desire an ice cream cone right now, but I do not hope for one: it's just (in my view) too trivial for that. (When I was five, I did hope for ice cream, because in my child's world it was really important! Adults, too, sometimes hope for things that are truly trivial—a victory for one's favorite sports team, for example—but subjectively they think this of enormous importance, like the child with the ice cream.)

My ice cream example brings me to a further issue: hope, like fear, always involves significant powerlessness. Right now, I desire a bottle of water. And if I felt like going to the basement where the vending machines are, I would get one. Sooner or later I will. But I don't *hope* for a bottle of water: that would suggest that I am somehow unable to get it myself, or that I am used to being waited on by rather unreliable people.

The ancient Greeks and Romans understood all three of these points, so they did not make the mistake of defining hope in terms of desire and probability. Instead, they said that hope was the cousin, or flip side, of fear. Both involve evaluation of an outcome as very important, both involve great uncertainty about the outcome, and both involve a good measure of passivity or lack of control. They therefore did not like hope, pleasant though they granted it was: hope betrays a mind too dependent on fortune. "You will cease to fear, if you cease to hope," writes Seneca. "Both belong to a soul that is hanging in suspense, to a soul that is made anxious by concern with the future" (*Moral Epistles*, 5.7–8).[5]

I've already rejected the Stoic position that we should insulate ourselves from painful shocks by not caring greatly about anything outside ourselves. The Stoic view removes too much, leaving no love of family or country, nothing really to make life worth living. But if we keep deep love, then we are stuck with fears and hopes—and at times with profound grief. So, we should reject the Stoic dismissal of both hope and fear. But we should acknowledge that they are correct that the two are cousins. Where you fear, there too you will hope.

What, then, *is* the difference between the two? The Stoics call hopes "sweet delights," and they know that fear feels awful. They also use metaphors like "expansion" and "uplift" when talking about hope, whereas fear goes with "contraction" and shrinking. We talk this way, too: hope has wings, it has feathers like a bird, it soars upward. Horror movie soundtracks know how to whip up fear musically. The music of hope is totally different. (I think of Vaughan Williams's frail and lovely "The Lark Ascending" (1914), expressing hope for Europe in the perilous days before the First World War. But there is hope music in every musical genre.) So, the two emotions differ, clearly, in the characteristic feelings that attend them and in

[5]I study many more examples of this view, from Seneca and others, in my *The Therapy of Desire: Theory and Practice in Hellenistic Ethics* (Princeton: Princeton University Press, 1994, updated edition 2009).

[illegible]ior of the person affected by them. Hope swells out-[illegible]ear shrinks back.

But if they have basically the same idea—namely, that a valued outcome is uncertain—and if it isn't the probabilities that make the difference, what *is* the difference in the person's thoughts and attitudes that results in (or is accompanied by) this difference of feeling? It appears that the difference is one of focus. It's like the glass is half empty, the glass is half full. The same glass, a different focus of vision. In fear, you focus on the bad outcome that may occur. In hope, you focus on the good.

A recent book by philosopher Adrienne Martin, called *How We Hope: A Moral Psychology*,[6] adds a very important point. Hope, Martin argues, is more like a "syndrome" than just an attitude or emotion: it includes thoughts, imaginings, preparations for action, even actions. I don't see this as peculiar to hope; fear also has strong connections to imagination and action. But what are the actions and thoughts characteristic of hope? I'd say that hope involves a vision of the good world that might ensue, and, often at least, actions related to getting there. Some of these might be similar to the actions prompted by fear, since warding off a bad possibility can be very similar to promoting a good one. Fear of danger, when it is proportional and healthy, prompts evasive strategies that can make safety and health more likely. Still, there is a difference. The patient who is full of fear may become paralyzed; a hopeful patient may be more energetic in seeking solutions. And maybe, though we

[6]Above, n. 4.

still know too little about this, the hope itself is efficacious. Th placebo effect shows that at least in many situations, thinking one is going to get better produces real improvement. Hope does not rest on such probabilistic beliefs, as I've said, but it might be similarly effective.

Martin's idea about the connection between hope and positive action is powerful, but hope does not always work this way. Sometimes hoping is inert and impotent, and may even distract from useful work. In academic life we all know people who live in hope: they hope that someday they will write something good, they imagine themselves reading a fine article that they have produced, they see it set in type in the pages of the *Journal of Philosophy*, etc. But that sort of thing can be self-indulgent fantasy or even a substitute for getting down to work. In such cases we would be right to prefer the person who works without any particular emotional attitude to the person who indulges in emotion and fantas without work.

We need, then, to distinguish, as Martin does not, betwee what we might call "idle hope" and what we might call "practical hope," hope that is firmly linked to, and that energizes a commitment to action. But while idle hope surely exists, hope can often be truly practical: the beautiful imaginings and fantasies involved in hoping can energize action toward the valuable goal. It's hard to sustain commitment to a difficult struggle without such energizing thoughts and feelings. The difference between fearing and hoping is slender. It's like flipping a switch: now the glass looks half full. And these mental

images, often at least, do important practical work, preparing me to take action toward the valuable goal and convincing me that it's within reach.

That's what I was doing, I guess, on June 15: in the face of a drumbeat of bad news, summoning up things to focus on that are beautiful and good and connected to valuable goals of constructive work and reconciliation, with the result that I became more serene and unwavering in my ongoing pursuit of those goals.

HOPE AS A "PRACTICAL POSTULATE"

Why on earth should we hope? The world does not give us reasons for that attitude. And I've already said that hope is not a matter of probability calculation. There is always a choice: Which images shall I focus on? What thoughts shall I summon up in my mental space?

One reason for hoping is the likely placebo effect: sometimes hope in and of itself can make the good outcome more likely. But there's no placebo effect in politics: hoping that person P or legislation L will make America great again, or improve your employment or health situation, doesn't by itself make those results more likely. So why not just be glum and cynical, expecting the worst? There is less disappointment that way. This sounds suspiciously like the Stoic view: don't care about uncertain things too much. And we already said that this was bad because it means renouncing love, whether of people or of a country. If you focus fearfully, ahead of time, on the possible failure of your marriage, what sort of marriage could that be? So, a first reason for hope is that it keeps love and trust alive, and love is valuable.

A further argument was made by Immanuel Kant. Kant believed that we have a duty, during our lives, to engage in actions that produce valuable social goals—actions that make it more likely that human beings will treat one another as ends, not as mere instruments. (Central in his own thinking was the aim of producing world peace.[7]) But Kant also understood, and plainly felt in his heart, that when we look around us it is difficult to sustain our own efforts: we see so much bad behavior, so much hatred, human beings everywhere falling so far short of what we might wish human beings to be and do. He said that if we asked our own hearts the question, "Is the human race as a whole likeable, or is it an object to be regarded with distaste?" we just don't know what to say. (Among the other evils Kant attacks are arbitrary monarchy, the slave trade, self-aggrandizing nationalism, and the absence of religious freedom and the freedom of speech.[8])

[7]His last published work was *Perpetual Peace* (1795), but he discussed this goal extensively in earlier works as well.

[8]*Perpetual Peace* attacks the slave trade, colonial domination, and aggressive nationalism; it also comments as forcefully as Kant could in his time about the great importance of allowing extensive freedom of speech and debate: the "Secret Article" of a perpetual peace among nations is that philosophers will be able to publish works advocating it! His ideas about religion are most extensively discussed in *Religion Within the Limits of Mere Reason* (1793), reference above ch. 5; here Kant advocates a rationalistic Enlightenment religion of the Deistic sort (and also resembling a

But if we ought to be pursuing valuable social goals, then we ought to motivate ourselves to pursue them—and this means embracing hope. So, Kant concludes that we should choose hope as what he calls a "practical postulate," an attitude that we take on without sufficient reasons, for the sake of the good action it may enable.

> However uncertain I may be and may remain as to whether we can hope for anything better for mankind, this uncertainty cannot detract from the maxim I have adopted, or from the necessity of assuming for practical purposes that human progress is possible. This hope for better times to come, without which an earnest desire to do something useful for the common good would never have inspired the human heart, has always influenced the activities of right-thinking people.[9]

Kant is right: good works need hope. When you have a child, you have no idea, really, what sort of person your child will become, or what sort of life he or she will have. But you know that you want to be a good parent: so, you embrace hope. Practical hope, not idle hope, since you get to work to produce a good future for your child. But could you do that without hope?

---

rationalistic Judaism, as his friend Moses Mendelssohn pointed out), but he insists on complete freedom of religions belief and practice.

[9]Kant, from the essay "On the Common Saying: That May Be True in Theory, But It Is of No Use in Practice" (often called "Theory and Practice"), see *Kant's Political Writings*, ed. Hans Reiss (Cambridge: Cambridge University Press, 1991), 90.

Kant says plausibly that you could not. When you love a cause, or a country, once again you need to embrace hope to sustain you in your efforts on its behalf. Think of Martin Luther King Jr., of Gandhi, of the Founders of the United States, of Nelson Mandela—all people of hope and vision, who saw a beautiful future and worked energetically to realize it. Despair, or even cynical resignation, are attitudes incompatible with bold action and committed work.

We're talking about people committed to genuinely good causes. Hope itself is neutral: criminals have hope, dictators, tax evaders, fanatics of all sorts have hope. Indeed, we wish these people didn't have so much high hope, since they might then be less energetic in pursuing their bad goals. A languid, timorous Hitler would probably have done little damage to the world, whereas the hopeful visionary Hitler did untold damage. I'm saying that hope is crucial to the energetic pursuit of a difficult goal. And then, *if* the goal is a genuinely valuable one, and *if* we agree with Kant that we ought to live in a way that promotes genuinely valuable goals, we have a very powerful reason to embrace hope.

Hope really is a choice, and a practical habit. Any human situation, any marriage, any job, any friendship, is always a mixture of good and bad. How we engage with it often depends on our emotional focus. You can always say to yourself, "This is terrible, and I am miserable," focusing on the ways in which that part of your life fails to meet your ideal. Or you can say, "This is pretty great," focusing on the part that really is great. Similarly, facing the future, you can say, "This is likely to be a mess," and face the future with fear. Or you can say, "This can be really wonderful." And then you embrace hope for the future of that friendship, or that job.

HOPE, THE OPPOSITE OF FEAR

We've said from the start that hope is the opposite or flip side of fear. Both react to uncertainty, but in opposing ways. Their action tendencies are for that reason very different. Hope expands and surges forward, fear shrinks back. Hope is vulnerable, fear self-protective. Of course, it is likely that everyone will have pockets of fear even amid hope: I can be hopeful for my children, my friendships, my family, and yet fearful about my health or the health of a friend. So, what we are talking about here is the difference between hope and fear *directed at the same goal*, in this case the future of my country in its efforts toward justice and flourishing. Directed at the same outcomes, hope and fear are extremely different, and it really is like flipping a switch: I can't hope and fear for the same thing at the same time (although I can certainly oscillate between periods of hope and periods of fearfulness).

I've said from the beginning that fear is connected to the monarchical desire to control others rather than to trust them to be independent and themselves. Similarly, a the person who refuses to hope for the future is likely to be a controlling sort of person, what I've called a monarchical person: nothing is good unless it dovetails entirely with my wishes, with no pockets of uncertainty and vulnerability. No hope here, because I don't have the entirety of what I want, and I don't want to depend on other unreliable people, or on chance. The spirit of hope, then, is obscurely linked to a spirit of respect for the independence of others, to a renunciation of monarchical ambition, a kind of relaxation and expansion of the heart. The Stoics said that hope was "expansion," and "uplift." Poets connect hope with soaring and flying. The Indian poet-philosopher Rabindranath Tagore once said of a young woman getting married that she was "stepping into the waters of chance, unafraid."[10] That's what hope involves.

Put in political terms, democracy surely involves some fear, and fear can be a useful guide in many areas of democratic life, when the underlying facts are right. Fear of terrorism, fear of unsafe highways and bridges, fear of the loss of freedom itself: all of these can prompt useful protective action. But directed to the very future of the democratic project itself, a fearful approach is likely to be dangerous, leading people to seek autocratic control, or the protection of someone who will control outcomes for them. Martin Luther King Jr. understood that a fearful approach to the future of race relations would play straight into the hands of those who sought to manage things by violence, a kind of preemptive strike. His emphasis on hope was an attempt to flip the switch, getting people to dwell mentally on good outcomes that could come about through peaceful work and cooperation.

On June 15, I threw myself into the waters of chance, reinforcing my commitment to some totally uncertain things and

[10]Poem written to his former pupil the late Amita Sen (mother of economist Amartya Sen), hanging still in her home in Santiniketan, West Bengal.

embracing them, with a vision of how the world could be: as King says, "a world where men and women can live together." We have to do this every day, if we are really serious about the pursuit of difficult and noble goals. Crazy, but, as Kant says, necessary.

HOPE'S RELATIVES: FAITH AND LOVE

Hope is closely connected to two other emotional attitudes: faith and love. Christian thought traditionally links these three, and Saint Paul adds that the greatest of the three is love. Martin Luther King Jr. follows Christian teaching by linking the three attitudes, albeit not in a theistic and theological way, but in a this-worldly way that embraces all Americans.[11]

Why faith, then? And what could King have meant, what can we mean today, by this-worldly faith? I said that hope does not rest on probabilities, and indeed is pretty independent of any specific attitude as to how likely the outcome is. Not entirely independent, however. We need to believe that the good things we hope for are have a realistic chance of being realized through the efforts of flawed human beings. If we think that justice is possible only in heaven, this inhibits our efforts in this life. So, King had to go against one strand in the Christian tradition, urging his followers to have this-worldly faith that

[11]See *A Testament of Hope* (reference in ch. 3) for hundreds of examples of these connections.

what they were doing, protesting and marching, could actually bear fruit, and preferably in their lifetimes. Otherwise, hard work and risk-taking action seem not worth it. So too with us today. If we think that democratic politics has gone down the drain and that our efforts are a waste of time, we won't embrace hope.

Faith of this sort does not need to be, and should not be, utopian or unrealistic. We may *not* believe that the goal will be accomplished quickly, and we may not even think that it will be fully realized in our time, but we probably need to think that meaningful progress is a plausible expectation if we work hard. But the goal itself must not be conceived in an unrealistic way, as a type of perfect justice that human beings can't sustain. Such hopes all too often lead to cynicism or despair. Real human beings and real human life are what we need to believe in, and that means that hope, bolstered by faith, needs to embrace something that flawed human beings are capable of and might really do.

Think of King's speech again. The "I Have a Dream" speech is soaring idealistic poetry, expressing faith in a beautiful goal and asking us all to embrace that goal with hope. But what does King actually ask us to imagine? Only this: that in Georgia, "the sons of former slaves and the sons of former slave owners will be able to sit down together at the table of brotherhood." Not that they will agree with one another in all respects, not that systemic racism will be a thing of the past: only that people will sit down together to talk. That, in our own time, is real. Only this: that in Alabama, "little black boys and black girls will be able to join hands with little white boys and white girls as sisters and brothers." That doesn't happen 100 percent of the time, obviously, but it can happen, and often does happen, right there in Alabama. So that too, in our own time, is real, and made dramatically real in December 2017 by the election of Democrat Doug Jones to the Senate, defeating racist Roy Moore—thanks in large part to the vigorous support of African American voters, newly empowered. King asks us to believe in the possibility of small daily human acts of brotherhood, not a perfect world. The real is made beautiful, and that is what hope embraces. Utopianism is a forerunner of despair, so faith and hope need to find beauty in the near.

So too with my thoughts on June 15. My hope and its accompanying faith remain indefinite, as they had better do, but the things on which they focus—better lives for African American young people on the South Side of Chicago, at least some good legislative deliberations about the common good, are surely just as possible as the changes King envisaged in the deep South. The Danny Maseng song asks for a new loving spirit, committed to building bridges, and that is surely difficult—but I don't need to believe that everyone will love everyone all the time, just often enough to make a difference. So: hope needs faith, but faith need not be, and had better not be, based on an unrealistic view of people.

There's a more subtle kind of faith that we need in human relations. If faith is, as Saint Paul said, "the evidence of things not seen," then we need faith any time we engage with another person in a more than casual way. We need, that is, to treat that other person as a person, having depth and an inner life, a point of view on the world, and emotions similar to our own.

What we see is just a shape, moving and making sounds. Even before automata were a reality, people made up stories about them: they even appear in Homer's *Iliad*. People were fascinated by the inscrutability of the other, so they wondered how to tell a real person from such a machine. The answer is there is no way to tell: we have to go on faith. Through stories, novels, and poems we learn how to endow a human form with humanity, and we quickly form the habit of doing so. But it isn't automatic, and it always requires a type of generosity that goes beyond the evidence. This sort of faith, crucial in personal love and friendship, we also need in political life. We need to think of our opponents as having capacities for reasoning and a range of human emotions, whether badly developed and used or not.

What about love? Love comes in many types, and we surely do not have to have romantic love for our political opponents, or even the reciprocal liking characteristic of friendly love. (King said this countless times so that he would not be misunderstood.) But there is a type of love that is closely linked to the faith I've just described, a love that simply consists in seeing the other person as fully human, and capable at some level of good and of change.

If you don't have love for others, then the life of Stoic detachment or even cynical despair will make more sense than the life of hope, with its many demands. So, there is a kind of base-level of love that is needed, even before people take an interest in hope. But as habits of hope develop, they are sustained by, and further sustain, habits of love, a generosity of spirit that practices seeing good in others and expecting good things, rather than expecting the worst. As King often noted, this sort of love is assisted by learning to separate the doer from the deed. Deeds may be denounced unequivocally. People are always larger than their deeds, capable of growth and change.

It would be hard to find a person in politics who had seen more human evil than Nelson Mandela. Oppressed for most of his life by the brutal racism of South African apartheid, imprisoned for twenty-seven years, much of that in deplorable conditions on Robben Island, he saw a lot of human badness. And yet, throughout his life Mandela remained a man of hope, faith, and love. In prison he struggled against mental bitterness and toward hope by thinking about how people were capable of working together for good ends. He meditated on such things in a habitual way. He cultivated understanding of his oppressors by learning the Afrikaans language.[12]

All of this led to a remarkable demeanor in politics, one that always did separate the doer from the deed, showing that he believed in the good possibilities inherent in all. And such was the power of his generous and hopeful demeanor, he actually elicited such behavior, more often than not. As his funeral procession wound through the streets, a white police officer, tears running down his cheeks, recalled how Mandela had been driven through the streets on the occasion of his inauguration as president in 1994. His car passed by a group of young police recruits, including the speaker, who said he was

[12]Two indispensable sources for Mandela's thought are his autobiography, *Long Walk to Freedom* (Boston: Back Bay Books, 1994), and a book of interviews and letters, which (following the Stoic philosopher Marcus Aurelius) he entitled *Conversations with Myself* (London: MacMillan, 2010).

expecting only hatred and scorn. Mandela got down from his car and shook the hands of all the young men, smiling his winning smile and saying, "Our trust is in you."[13] Again and again, the warmth of his personality moved people to the core: the coach and players of the national rugby team (well depicted in the movie *Invictus*), the chief of South African security, even the jailer who had to cook for him in his final prison, more like a hotel (since it was clear by then that he would be president).[14] Feeling that they were seen as capable of good, people usually tried to live up to that expectation.

Mandela's stance combined our three attitudes. During a long, dark period, with an uncertain future, he embraced hope. He did so, it seems, through an unwavering faith in the prospects of his troubled nation, not for perfect justice, but for the ultimate rejection of apartheid in favor of multiracial democracy. At its deepest level, though, both faith and hope were sustained by Mandela's almost heroic capacity for love: for seeing the potential for good in his fellow countrymen, white and black and embracing them in the light of that possibility.

Mandela is a heroic figure, but we don't have to aspire to that extraordinary generosity in adversity. We just need to move in that direction, and we can do that right now, today—getting in the habit of seeing people who thwart us not as

[13]CNN coverage of Mandela's funeral.

[14]John Carlin's *Invictus: Nelson Mandela and the Game That Made a Nation* (New York: Penguin, 2008), originally called *Playing the Enemy* with the same subtitle, is the source for the film, but has a lot more material; it contains many of these anecdotes; others are described by Mandela himself in his two autobiographical works.

monsters but as thinking and feeling real people who are not totally evil.

I notice this in my extended family, where there are large political differences. I find that the very fact that people basically love me means that they do not trash my arguments in the way that they are used to trashing arguments from others on the left. Now, of course, this movement from love into some sort of listening and exchange is fragile: the vitriol might spill back into the family love, tainting and spoiling it. I'm sure this happens often. But the opposite possibility exists, and we can cultivate it: from a vision of a person as real and potentially lovable, we can get to the hope for a real dialogue.

Let's think again, now, about disgust. Mandela seems to have been unusually free of bodily disgust. Thus, he volunteered to dispose of wastes in the Robben Island prison when one of his fellow prisoners could not bear to do it. This acceptance of the body may have helped him avoid projecting disgust onto any people or group, including racist whites. Projective disgust is a denial of love and faith. It says, "This is an animal, not a full human being." Racist South Africans said that all the time, and it would have been easy for Mandela to reciprocate. But he always preserved his faith that behind the looming shapes of his oppressors were real human feelings and many aims for good, despite the bad deeds. Political hope requires putting disgust on hold.

It's easy to say this in theory, difficult to achieve it. Many of my students are full of disgust at Trump and Trump supporters, and many of my academic colleagues are, too. Nor do they imagine the full humanity of those human beings, or separate their deeds from the person behind the deeds. As Mandela and King show us, we can unequivocally condemn racism without viewing racists as irremediably evil. As long as we see one another this way, we won't have faith in future good emerging, and we won't have the sort of love that envisages possibilities of cooperation and brotherhood. And that means that we will not follow Kant's advice and embrace hope.

What practices relevant to good citizenship might we encourage, as we seek to flip the switch from fear to hope—and, in particular, hope connected to constructive work and bridge-building dialogue? Early in this chapter I asked myself what institutions in our society gave me, personally, reasons for hope. Here I'm asking a different but related question: what are, so to speak, the schools of hope, areas of our common life that we should encourage and strengthen on the grounds that they help people sustain or embrace hope? Much of the work of sustaining or building hope is done in families and in personal friendships of many kinds. But there are five, at least, that we can look to as we try to sustain hope for a decent future: poetry, music, and the other arts; critical thinking (in schools, universities, and adult discussion groups of many kinds); religious groups insofar as they practice love and respect for others; solidarity groups focused on securing justice in a non-violent and dialogical way; and (often closely connected to such groups) theories of what justice is, accounts of the goal that we can focus on to enrich our efforts. Each "practice" has bad as well as good exemplars, but each contains huge potential for a hopeful future.

I'll argue, though, that all ought to be supplemented by a sixth "practice" of citizenship: a national service program required of all young people that would put young citizens into close contact with people different in age, ethnicity, and economic level, in the context of constructive service. Politically unpopular as it no doubt is, I believe that this solution is urgently important.

PRACTICES OF HOPE: THE ARTS

First, let's deepen a theme that formed part of Winnicott's account of mature concern and of my own anti-disgust proposal. Walt Whitman, who might be called our national poet, said that "these states" need poets, because the poet is "the arbiter of the diverse," "the equalizer of his age and land" ("By Blue Ontario's Shore," section 10). What Whitman meant is that poets have the professional habit of love in the sense that I have described it: that is, they see whatever they see as full, real, and infinitely complex, and as separate from the ego. Love in this sense is anti-narcissistic, determined to cede an area of mystery and infinite complexity to each "other," and determined to let each speak, act, and be. "He sees eternity in men and women, he does not see men and women as dreams or dots," says Whitman, implicitly contrasting his poems of America with other more bureaucratic practices. A runaway slave is fully present as a real and complex, feeling person. A woman's desire for freedom is present too, and the gay man's longing for fulfillment. Other discourses useful to politics, Whitman suggests, do not contain this sense of boundless richness, so if all we read is, say, economic treatises, we risk losing something precious about the humanity of human beings.

Artists may of course have a blinkered or mistaken political vision. Some have been sexist, some anti-Semitic, some racist. Whitman is not saying that art is unerring. He is saying, instead, that insofar as the poet does engage poetically with a human being, exploring those mysterious insides and inviting us to do so, thus far the poet offers a practice for democratic citizenship.

This theme has been developed by many literary artists. African American novelist Ralph Ellison, in a later introductory essay about his great novel *Invisible Man*, described his novel as "a raft of hope, perception, and entertainment" on which America's democracy may "negotiate the snags and whirlpools" that stand between us and "the democratic ideal."[15] The image of the raft is a rich one, alluding to the trip down the Mississippi taken by Huck Finn and the slave Jim, during which each learns something of how the world looks through the other's eyes and grows to see the other not as a looming shape or inert body, but as a reservoir of human thoughts and feelings.

Ellison's novel is, centrally, a novel about vision and blindness. His hero, an unnamed African American, opens the novel by saying, "I am an invisible man." He then explains that he is not a ghost. He has a body, and "might even be said to possess a mind." He is invisible simply "because people refuse to see me." It's as if he is surrounded by mirrors in which

[15]Ralph Waldo Ellison, "Introduction," *Invisible Man* (New York: Vintage, 1995), xx–xxi.

people see only "my surroundings, themselves, or figments of their imagination—everything and anything except me." Why? "That invisibility to which I refer occurs because of a peculiar disposition of the eyes of those with whom I come in contact. A matter of the construction of their inner eyes, those eyes with which they look through their physical eyes on reality."[16] Ellison's novel addresses the inner eyes of its mainly white readership, not through sentimentality or easy empathy, but through scorching satire, fantastic hyperbolic humor, all in the service of a deeper and more difficult sympathy. What Ellison's later essay suggests is that the insight is inseparable from the fictional craft.

Let me give just one more example of this theme. Israeli novelist David Grossman, the 2017 winner of the Man Booker International Prize, gave a speech at the graduation ceremony at Hebrew University on June 11, 2017, addressing the role of the novelist in a profoundly divided society. (He was receiving an honorary doctorate, as was I, and had been invited to reply on behalf of all the honorees. He spoke in Hebrew, with simultaneous English translation.) Grossman said that his creative profession offers "the possibility of touching infinity"—not some heavenly infinity, but the infinite complexity, that "wholeness—made up of infinite flaws, with defects and deficiencies of both mind and body," the "endless possibilities and ways of being inside life" that characterize any single human being. He then described his painful struggle to understand and convey one of his most famous characters (Ora,

[16]Ibid., 3.

the heroine of Grossman's much-praised novel *To the End of the Land*).[17] He felt that he was trying to get at her psyche, but there was a blockage. Eventually, he came to understand that the problem was his own desire for total control, his desire to impose a meaning on a separate life. Finally, he understood: "it was not Ora who had to submit to me, but I who had to submit to her. In other words, I had to stop resisting the possibility of Ora inside me." This sense of openness and vulnerability before the infinite complexity of the human, Grossman suggests, is an author's gift to his nation. (His prize-winning new novel, *A Horse Walks into a Bar*, is another tour de force of imaginative surrender, as its narrator, a guilt-ridden, cynical stand-up comic, speaks from inside Grossman in a scathing, relentless, almost unendurable voice, with satire even darker than Ellison's.)

At that point, the speech turned political, as Grossman expressed his sense that this openness to the full humanity of each person is in grave danger of getting lost in divided Israel, anxious, fear-ridden, full of emotions that block that vision and that vulnerability. He continued in this vein, as many in the audience began booing. At the end, a mere handful gave him a standing ovation—about ten of the hundred PhD graduates, two of the eleven other honorees (a Belgian physicist and I), and almost nobody in the audience. That response, however, does not show that Grossman's work and work of other

[17]*To the End of the Land* (2008) is generally regarded as his most important achievement. All quotes from his speech are from an official English translation given me courtesy of the author; I have on file both Hebrew and English versions.

artists is not a school of hope. Hope often has to begin with a few. And in our own nation, let's hope that fear and blame have not encroached upon hope as far as in today's Israel. Let's hope. And clearly, it's not fluff that we need or even just high-level but easy novels of empathy, such as *To Kill a Mockingbird*. Ellison was right: the "raft" has to negotiate "snags and whirlpools," so it had better be difficult, often dark, provoking protest and discomfort as well as tears and gratitude. And the novelist has to be alert to the possibility of a cooptation by causes that would corrupt his or her voice. Ellison was accused, I think wrongly, of allowing himself to become the mascot of liberal whites. Grossman will have to watch out lest he become the mascot of those (in Europe especially) who just hate Israel and want the worst rather than the best.

I've spoken of poetry and novels. These go to work on our inner eyes in moments of solitary contemplation. But we also need experiences of art in which we are kinetic and active, engaged in making something together. When people come together to sing or dance, or to act a play together, or even to sing along with the CD of *Hamilton* together, as so many kids do, they share breath and bodily contact with one another, promoting a sense of common work and joy. And public works of sculpture and visual art can also involve us in making beauty together, or sharing a sense of the comic vulnerability of bodies. People who visit Chicago's Millennium Park wade in the pool between the two large screens of Jaume Plensa's Crown Fountain, seeing on the screens those huge faces of Chicagoans of different ages and races, moving in comic slow motion—and eagerly awaiting the moment when, as if out of the mouth of each face, a jet of cool water sprays out, wetting the waders. Water is a potent metaphor in our divided racial history. The invitation to have fun being sprayed on "by" a face of a different race or gender includes us all in miscegenation, creating images of how our bitter racial divisions might possibly be overcome.

Some nations come together through a sense of ethnic homogeneity, a perilous way to connect in an era of migration. Our nation has always imagined itself as peopled by many different groups. But overcoming fear and suspicion in the direction of real cooperation has never come easily, and the arts offer bridges to seeing human diversity as joyful, funny, tragic, delightful, not as a horrible fate to be shunned.

PRACTICES OF HOPE: THE SPIRIT OF SOCRATES

Socrates said that democracy was "a noble but sluggish horse," and that he was like a "gadfly," waking it up with his sting.[18] His sting was the demand for rigorous and critical self-examination. Most people then, as now, had a lot of basically good beliefs, and Socrates's entire method relied on this. But

[18]Plato, *Apology*, 30 E. (These marginal numbers from a Renaissance edition appear in virtually all translations and give uniformity to references.) As in chapter 1, by "Socrates" I mean the Platonic character in a group of what are standardly called "early dialogues," which are standardly taken to represent the historical practice of Socrates, who was, unlike Plato, a democrat, though one who favored a larger role for critical thinking than Athens then allowed. (All offices except that of general were filled by lottery.)

Athenian democrats, like modern Americans, were careless, hasty, prone to overconfident boasting and to substituting invective for argument. The result was, and is, that people don't know what they really believe: they just have not stopped to sort this out.

The people Socrates questioned also had bad ways of relating to others, connected to their self-obtuseness. They approach interaction like a contest of boasting, and sought prestige by defeating their "opponents" in debate. They talked a lot, and listened little. Their voices were loud, angry, overconfident. It's no accident that the later Stoic philosopher Marcus Aurelius compared political discourse to a sports match, in which people were cheering for their own team, but nobody was seeking the truth.

Socratic reasoning is a practice of hope because it creates a world of listening, of quiet voices, and of mutual respect for reason. Its participants already share a goal: to get the argument right. Both Laches and Nicias really want to understand what courage is, not simply to make up some flashy tale about courage. I keep remembering a young college student I interviewed back in 1994 or so, when I was writing my book *Cultivating Humanity*, about required liberal arts courses. This student—whom I met because he was working behind the desk in my gym—attended a local business college that required all students to take some philosophy courses. He told me he found it really intriguing to be asked to reconstruct the arguments of political speeches and newspaper editorials, detecting fallacies, or ambiguous or false premises. But the biggest surprise came when the class staged debates on issues of the day, and he was assigned the job of arguing against the death penalty, although he actually supported it. He told me he had had no idea, before that, that you could produce arguments for a position you did not hold. (What a black mark for our media culture, that he had not gotten this idea, although he is a very smart person.) That effort to come up with what the other side would say, he told me, changed his whole attitude to political debate. Now he is more likely to respect the "other side" and to be curious about their reasoning. When the arguments are laid out, it may turn out that both sides share some premises, and we can understand where differences kick in.

Our media culture is even more hostile to Socrates than the talk radio culture of 1994. Social media encourage brief blurts of opinion, rather than the working out of a complex argument. The tone is often shrill, as if people are shouting to be heard. People don't listen: everything is me me me. Attention spans, already shortened by many aspects of our technology (constant phone checking, distracted walking and driving) become even shorter, since social media encourage the thought that everything worth saying can be said right away, in a trumpet of self-proclamation. So where do we find these Socratic practices of hope?

They still flourish, usually, in the liberal arts programs of our colleges and universities. I have worries, since there is an increasing unwillingness to listen to uncomfortable challenges and a desire to insulate the classroom so that it contains only ideas that students already hold. This demand for safety rather than challenge and critique comes primarily from students, and it should be resisted. I co-teach with my most conservative colleague, the well-known blogger Will Baude—also one of the best young scholars of constitutional law—in order to model a Socratic commitment that truly crosses our political divides. Of course, the classroom should be civil, and debate must not vilify or demean. But that does not mean silencing uncomfortable ideas.

Philosophy departments still practice the Socratic virtues for the most part, and some of our top philosophy publishers have encouraged the preparation of "pro and con" books for students that open up difficult issues in an attractive and civil way. Among other such books, one can find a valuable discussion of climate change in *Debating Climate Ethics* by Stephen M. Gardiner and (my colleague) David A. Weisbach (Oxford University Press); of the limits of religious exemptions from nondiscrimination laws in *Debating Religious Liberty and Discrimination*, by Ryan T. Anderson, John Corvino, and Sherif Girgis (Oxford University Press); in *Debating Same-Sex Marriage*, by John Corvino and Maggie Gallagher (Oxford University Press); in *Libertarianism: For and Against*, by Craig Duncan and Tibor Machan (Rowman and Littlefield). We should applaud these authors for sacrificing their time and often their professional search for prestige (since books aimed at teaching are not sources of prestige) in order to perform this public service. Two people who deserve special mention (as examples, and among many) are the philosopher John Corvino, who, a gay man and a first-rate philosopher, travels all over the country debating conservative opponents with good humor, wit, and excellent arguments; and, his opposite number, the great scholar of Jewish thought David Novak, who cheerfully enters the fray against same-sex marriage and other liberal causes, often in venues where he will be very isolated and unpopular with the audience—again, with great good humor, civility, and friendliness. People with tenure don't have to do this sort of thing, and they are rewarded for it only by the satisfaction of practicing hope.

Outside the academy, where can Americans find Socrates? In Europe adults gravitate eagerly to philosophical cafés and public lectures. It always surprises me that I get around thirty people at a book talk in the United States, and regularly get four hundred or five hundred in the Netherlands—and those people are buying tickets! American adults do eagerly seek out continuing education classes in the humanities, and public libraries and bookstores (reinventing themselves for the Amazon era) increasingly feed our hunger for face-to-face conversation. But America is a country of wide spaces that inhibit connection, and I wish we could figure out strategies to draw people into dialogue outside of major urban centers. (The isolation of aging people who no longer drive is a large part of this problem, and let's hope that the era of the self-driving car will rapidly diminish isolation.) The best attempts on this problem I've seen have come from universities and colleges themselves, creating lecture series and seminars for their communities. Grand Valley State University in Michigan, to take just one example, has a very good debate-focused lecture series, in which a modest donation gives people, in addition, a chance to sit with the speaker in a special reception. Many public universities have similar programs designed to bring the "town" to the campus. This is no luxury; it is part of being a responsible educational institution in a democracy.

I'd add that churches and synagogues also have events that are philosophical and discussion-oriented, among the many events they sponsor. I lectured at Old St. Patrick's Church in Chicago in May, a beautiful Romanesque structure that is one of the few Chicago buildings predating the 1871 fire. Founded in 1846, the church, a bastion of Irish American culture, now hosts events of all types, including a vigorous group for gay and lesbian Catholics and a group for people in Jewish-Catholic marriages. But one of their commitments is to philosophy, and they draw a large diverse public to such discussions. My synagogue, with its Words and Music program and other philosophical events, does the same. This brings me to my next topic.

PRACTICES OF HOPE: RELIGION

Religions sustain people in many ways in the crises of life and often serve as sources of hope—not just hope of salvation, if the religion talks of salvation, but also hope for and in our lives with one another on this earth. Let me return to Immanuel Kant, who said that we all have a duty to embrace hope in order to sustain our actions toward love of others, morality, and justice. Kant also thought that it was very difficult to sustain commitment to these goals in isolation; in a group with like-minded other people it was easier. So, he also said that everyone has a duty to join such a group. He thought that this group had to be a church, united by some type of belief in a higher power.

A man of the eighteenth century, Kant was not very fond of traditional religion. He thought it all too often divided people and encouraged immoral actions. So, he thought that the right type of church had to contain a good infusion of Socratic critical argument, to stop people from blindly following authority, and get them to think for themselves. But he did think that hope was best promoted by a church of the right sort, rather than, say, by civic or social groupings.

Kant made some bad mistakes, I think. He was too insistent on religious rationalism, scorning the many ways people connect to good principles through intuition, emotion, and faith. And while he was correct to see big dangers in religious authority, he was wrong to spurn it altogether; sometimes real people need worldly religious leaders. Finally, he was wrong about the connection between church and state: he thought the government should allow complete religious freedom but should subsidize only the sort of religion he liked, something that would be unacceptable in our democracy.

Still, Kant's basic point seems right. Hope and committed action are difficult in solitude, and religious groups are a primary way in which people find a hope-building and hope-sustaining community. It's no accident that my story of our city focused on the role of the black churches in sustaining hope at a very difficult time of racial division. Can we even imagine that the non-retributive and loving response of those members of the South Carolina church to the murders by white supremacist Dylan Roof, without thinking of people who attended church together regularly, and whose search for unconditional love was helped by the teaching of a pastor? In my story of my own synagogue, a demographically different and more privileged group, but one with all the conflicts and struggles of human life, of life in Chicago, and of life in America, the group played a key role in sustaining hope for many.

We should follow Kant to this extent: we should always ask ourselves where our religion is taking us and whether that goal is compatible with the love of all persons and a decent national future. But love often follows ritual routes that resonate deeply in memory, and we should be Socratic and skeptical only up to a point.

Philosophers sometimes show contempt for religion and religious people. That is one reason they have little public influence in our nation, a deeply religious nation. Our fellow citizens are not stupid or base to embrace religion. We must wish, and this seems as likely as anything good is likely, that each person who embraces religion will find there the ingredients of a hope that is inclusive and loving, rather than divisive and retributive. Philosophy by itself shows how we can respect our enemies; it does not show us how to love them. For that we need the arts, and many of us need religion.

PRACTICES OF HOPE: PROTEST MOVEMENTS

People who hope for justice and who want that hope to energize them toward justice usually need something more practical than religion (although it could be an outgrowth of religion). They need this-worldly movements that give them a sense of solidarity in a good cause. King knew that one of the great dangers for African Americans in racist America was despair. His movement beckoned to such people: join us, in pursuit of our dream. The women's movement, the gay rights movement, all have brought people formerly isolated into community around a set of goals, fostering hope.

As King knew well, movements come in many forms. His own hopeful nonviolent movement contended against the retributive and potentially violent movement of Malcolm X. Gandhi, similarly, contended against ideas of violent retribution advocated by the Hindu Right. He was assassinated by a member of that movement who believed that Gandhi had emasculated Hindu men by his opposition to retributive violence. Similar struggles have occurred in most large protest movements. As with religion, then, so here: we should endorse not the genus but the hope-oriented and reconciliation-oriented species. I think for the most part the Black Lives Matter movement has followed King, but there are segments that tend in the Malcolm X direction, and those do not foster hope or reconciliation. Similarly, the women's movement contains voices that demonize other feminists and seek to deny them a chance to speak—alongside more Socratic and inclusive voices. The gay rights movement has had some moments of hatred, but on the whole, has been exemplary for its unwavering defense of love against hate. The public celebration of love after the Orlando massacre, as hundreds of gays, lesbians, and friends and supporters turned out in the streets of Orlando to memorialize the dead—and to show that love is more powerful than hatred—is a vivid example of the way in which group membership can buttress hope.

Some movements toward justice are nationwide. Many

more are local. Grassroots organizing is perhaps one of our country's greatest and perennial resources in combatting fear and despair, and feeding hope.

PRACTICES OF HOPE: ACCOUNTS OF JUSTICE

People who hope for the future of their country need to have a vision of the goal for which they are striving. But it's a good idea to have more than a poetic vision. Here's another place where philosophy comes in handy in democratic life. Ever since Plato wrote the *Republic*, philosophers have created accounts of the just society, producing detailed arguments for these accounts and showing how a particular picture of the good or just society and its laws follows from assumptions that most people appear to accept. By now we have a wide variety of such accounts, of many different types: communitarian, Marxist, authoritarian, and liberal-social-democratic, and liberal-libertarian. For us in our time, although there is always much to be learned from theories that are radically different, what we need will be a theory that supports some type of liberal democracy—liberal in the sense of allowing ample freedoms of speech, press, and religion, and democracy in the sense of rule by the people, though this clearly doesn't rule out a large role for courts and administrative appointees, more indirectly accountable to the people.

But there are many different pictures of the just liberal-democratic state, and another thing liberal education often provides is the chance to understand, analyze, and debate these theories with other students. We should provide more public spaces where adults can do this, too. Theories differ greatly about what rights all citizens have (do these include social and economic rights, such as the right to health care?); about the right account of ownership and redistribution (how much taxation, for example, is compatible with a due respect for ownership?); and about the more precise definition of freedoms of religion, speech, and press, which our own Supreme Court constantly debates.

One theory among others is the "capabilities approach" to defining justice that I have worked on for years, co-founding an international association to promote further study and implementation. The basic idea of this approach is to define basic human entitlements in terms of the idea of "capabilities," or real opportunities that all citizens must have up to some acceptable threshold level, if the society in question is to count as even minimally just. I then attempt to justify a list of ten central "capabilities" that can be more concretely defined in each society. Here's the current list:

THE CENTRAL CAPABILITIES

1. LIFE. Being able to live to the end of a human life of normal length; not dying prematurely, or before one's life is so reduced as to be not worth living.
2. BODILY HEALTH. Being able to have good health, including reproductive health; to be adequately nourished; to have adequate shelter.

3. BODILY INTEGRITY. Being able to move freely from place to place; to be secure against violent assault, including sexual assault and domestic violence; having opportunities for sexual satisfaction and for choice in matters of reproduction.
4. SENSES, IMAGINATION, AND THOUGHT. Being able to use the senses, to imagine, think, and reason—and to do these things in a "truly human" way, a way informed and cultivated by an adequate education, including, but by no means limited to, literacy and basic mathematical and scientific training. Being able to use imagination and thought in connection with experiencing and producing works and events of one's own choice, religious, literary, musical, and so forth. Being able to use one's mind in ways protected by guarantees of freedom of expression with respect to both political and artistic speech, and freedom of religious exercise. Being able to have pleasurable experiences and to avoid non-beneficial pain.
5. EMOTIONS. Being able to have attachments to things and people outside ourselves; to love those who love and care for us, to grieve at their absence; in general, to love, to grieve, to experience longing, gratitude, and justified anger. Not having one's emotional development blighted by fear and anxiety. (Supporting this capability means supporting forms of human association that can be shown to be crucial in their development.)
6. PRACTICAL REASON. Being able to form a conception of the good and to engage in critical reflection about the planning of one's life. (This entails protection for the liberty of conscience and religious observance.)

7. AFFILIATION.

    A. Being able to live with and toward others, to recognize and show concern for other human beings, to engage in various forms of social interaction; to be able to imagine the situation of another. (Protecting this capability means protecting institutions that constitute and nourish such forms of affiliation, and also protecting the freedom of assembly and political speech.)
    B. Having the social bases of self-respect and nonhumiliation; being able to be treated as a dignified being whose worth is equal to that of others. This entails provisions of nondiscrimination on the basis of race, sex, sexual orientation, ethnicity, caste, religion, national origin.

8. OTHER SPECIES. Being able to live with concern for and in relation to animals, plants, and the world of nature.
9. PLAY. Being able to laugh, to play, to enjoy recreational activities.
10. CONTROL OVER ONE'S ENVIRONMENT.

    A. POLITICAL. Being able to participate effectively in political choices that govern one's life; having the right of political participation, protections of free speech and association.
    B. MATERIAL. Being able to hold property (both land and movable goods), and having property rights on an equal basis with others; having the right to seek employment on an equal basis with others; having the freedom from

> unwarranted search and seizure. In work, being able to work as a human being, exercising practical reason and entering into meaningful relationships of mutual recognition with other workers.

The focus is on capabilities rather than actual functioning because the theory gives great importance to choice. People may choose to fast for religious reasons when ample food is available, but there is a great difference between fasting and starving. I think this theory is a good basis for constitutional principles. On some issues, especially the rights of people with disabilities, I've argued that it does better than John Rawls's famous theory, which is extremely powerful and distinguished across most of the terrain of justice.[19] So when I hope, I don't simply hope for justice, I focus on a theory I've worked on over the years, that has definite implications for what we should do. And I work to bring that about.

Even though most people are obviously not professional philosophers, all people are well advised, I think, to study the theoretical alternatives and debate them, figuring out what account of the political goal they think best. Many Americans

[19]See my *Frontiers of Justice: Disability, Nationality, Species Membership* (Cambridge, MA: Harvard University Press, 2006). Earlier I developed the approach in *Women and Human Development: The Capabilities Approach* (New York: Cambridge University Press, 2000). A succinct general introduction to the approach, which also describes the contributions of other thinkers, is my *Creating Capabilities: The Human Development Approach* (Cambridge, MA: Harvard University Press, 2012). For Rawls's view, John Rawls, *A Theory of Justice* (Cambridge, MA: Harvard University Press, 1971).

right now don't agree with my view, which they will see as resembling European-style social democracy, for example, in its idea that health care is a basic social right. And it is notable that in Germany, where I often visit, even leading Conservative politicians urge the generous support not just for health care but also for disability care and education—it's part of what they think being Christian Democrats means, to care for the weak and for the family. When I was once asked to advise a subcommittee of the German national Bundestag, or Parliament, on development policy, I found that both left and right had really thought about norms with considerable sophistication and nuance. The right wing had, if anything, a more deeply philosophical orientation, asking me questions about Aquinas and other texts in normative political theory. If Germany right now, as I believe, is one of the more fear-resistant and balanced nations in Europe, it may well be because instead of snarky backbiting, politicians on both sides actually sit down and think.

I think it would be a good idea for all Americans—not just officials but also voters—to figure out what they really do think about such matters, prior to entering a contentious and difficult political debate. If hope focuses on a reasonably concrete picture of the just society, which one is prepared to defend with good arguments against alternative pictures, it is easier to advocate wisely for measures calculated to bring that goal about. And it is easier to see when compromises with the opposition are reasonable and when they jeopardize something intrinsic to justice itself.

THE IMPERATIVE OF NATIONAL SERVICE

So far, I have talked about ways of American life that already exist, although they can and should become more robust. But there is a large problem in American life that these "solutions" do not address. We live apart from one another. Most Americans, at least outside large urban centers, and often there, grow up in neighborhoods segregated by race and class. Gays and lesbians are now visible everywhere in American life because that identity cuts across those divisions; the same is true of people with disabilities. I believe that daily contact is a huge reason for the progress made by both of these movements. No comparable progress is found with race or class. (Gender is uniquely complex, since contact is intimate but true equality requires a change in the family, a major part of most people's lives.)

A second huge problem is that Americans lack a sense of the common good. They all too often think in narcissistic terms, what's good for me and for my family. This is nothing new: every democracy, both ancient and modern, has had to struggle against people's narrowness of vision and self-focus to create a meaningful narrative of common purpose. Some have done this through wars, but obviously that is not the most attractive way to come together or feel that we are all invested in one another.

The two problems are connected: because people don't meet one another across major divisions, they have a hard time thinking outside their economic or racial group toward a sense of common purpose.

I believe that a mandatory program of youth national civil service addresses both of these problems in an attractive and indeed necessary way. Modeled on the civil service arm of Germany's former national service requirement,[20] but entirely civil and for all young people, my program would enroll young people preferably for three years and send them to do work that urgently needs doing all over America: elder care, child care, infrastructure work, but always sending people into different regions, both geographically and economically. I don't have a detailed plan. Some suitable entrepreneur needs to do it, and since it is now politically unpopular, the first thing must be to sell it to people. The idea that we owe our country some of our work and our time is a very compelling idea if expressed well. The idea has roots in all the major religions and in secular ethics. In an era of shrinking government, we simply lack manpower to perform many essential services.

The subtext of my idea is that young people would see the diversity of people in their country, as soldiers in World War II learned to do during their service, only my young people would be trying to help, not to kill. In the course of those valuable acts of service they would also know the country in a new way. Stigma is typically founded on lack of close association; that's why the stigma attaching to gays and lesbians has diminished so rapidly with the coming-out of young people all over

[20]*Zivildienst* in Germany ended in 2011, along with military conscription; it was always viewed as an alternative to military service and thus was compulsory only for males.

the country. Now that same de-stigmatizing needs to happen, or happen more, with race, class—and also age.

People usually don't talk about national service because they assume it is politically impossible. But if people don't talk about it, it certainly won't be possible. So, I put my cards on the table.

WHY BOTHER WITH HOPE?

Stoicism and cynicism are perennial threats for the hopeful. The cynic scoffs at the romantic dreams of hopers.[21] The Stoic is less openly hostile but shrinks back from the waters of life into an insular detachment. Stoics promise us inner peace, proud independence, and a lofty superiority to fortune. Cynics say the world just isn't worth that much anyway.

Here I return to Cicero. His last work, *On Duties*, was written while he was moving from house to house in the country, trying to dodge assassins sent by Marc Antony, since Cicero was known to support the pro-republic, anti-empire conspiracy of Brutus and Cassius. (The assassins caught up to him shortly after that, slitting his throat.) In this work, addressed to his son (not an impressive young man, but his more intelligent daughter had recently died in childbirth), he defends the life of committed public service, with its hopes and its energetic efforts for the future. He admits that the detached hope-free life

[21]Here I mean the word *cynic* in its contemporary sense. The ancient Greek and Roman Cynics were close to the Stoics in their philosophical ideas.

has been chosen by "the noblest and most distinguished philosophers, and also certain strict and serious men who could not bear the conduct of the people or their leaders" (I.69). (This sounds to me all too familiar.) What they were after, he continues, is clearly appealing: "They wanted the same thing kings do: to need nothing, to obey nobody, to enjoy their liberty, which is defined as doing as you like."

Cicero is gentle with these people. He says that detachment from politics is understandable if people are in ill health, and even if they are immersed in some important intellectual pursuit. (His best friend Atticus was one of those detached people, so he had to create escape routes to express his love of his friend.) And Cicero knows well the pain of hopeful attachment: he often records in his letters his profound upset and grief about what he sees happening to the Roman Republic. The life of detachment is "easier and safer."

All the same, Cicero says, such people are guilty of what might be called "passive injustice": the injustice that consists in not energetically pursuing justice, even when that is very difficult. They also lack generosity and greatness of spirit. They do not serve the public good. In effect, Cicero is agreeing with Kant: we ought to serve the public good, so we had better become people who can stand to do that, not shrinking violets or the delicate unworldly sort of philosopher. Throughout his all-too-short life,[22] we see Cicero wrestling with his own fear,

[22]He was sixty-three when he was killed, but his work *On Old Age* makes it clear that the prototypical aging person, in his view, is eighty-something. To Atticus (three years older), he remarks that the two of them are not old

with fatigue, with stomach trouble, with the temptation to despair—and always coming out with renewed hope for committed service.

It's partly about justice, but, as we understand when we read what he has to say about Rome, it's mostly about love.

---

yet but will be getting there pretty soon. See the essay on Cicero in Nussbaum and Levmore, *Aging Thoughtfully*.

Acknowledgments

My first thanks are due to my colleagues at the University of Chicago Law School, who generously read sections of this manuscript for a faculty workshop and offered me challenging comments. Apart from Saul Levmore, to whom I am dedicating this book, I can single out Douglas Baird, LaToya Baldwin Clark, Nicolas Delon, Dhammika Dharmapala, Justin Driver, Tom Ginsburg, Todd Henderson, Aziz Huq, Alison LaCroix, Brian Leiter, Richard McAdams, David Weisbach, and Laura Weinrib. I profited greatly from discussion of envy and *Hamilton* with my colleague Will Baude (who had had a first child several days before the faculty workshop in question, otherwise he would have been on that list, too, for sure). I currently have three research assistants, all graduate students in the Philosophy Department (and one also a law student); all three have offered wonderful comments: Molly Brown, Emily Dupree, and Nethanel Lipshitz. Earlier I had two excellent RAs from the Law School, Scott Henney and Sophia Schloen. Thanks are also due to students in my courses over the years, particularly Emotions, Reason, and Law, where we have many spirited debates about all the emotions discussed here, and Feminist Philosophy, where I routinely try out my interpretation of Rousseau's *Emile*, and where, this year, I tried out some of the ideas in the misogyny chapter. I presented the envy chapter, which in fact was the first one I drafted, at a faculty-student workshop at Brown University, and received helpful comments from David Estlund, Sharon Krause, and Charles Larmore. Chapter 3 is close to my Jefferson Lecture given in May 2017 for the National Endowment for the Humanities, and I am grateful to the Endowment and to William Adams, then its chair, for challenging conversations (although, given the formality and the time constraints of the Kennedy Center venue, questions were unfortunately not permitted after the lecture itself). In addition to some of the colleagues named above, Ro Khanna and Charles Nussbaum read and commented on a draft of the Jefferson Lecture.

Nathaniel Levmore has been a totally undeferential companion in many good discussions of fear, anger, and envy. Eliot Levmore arranged for me to discuss anger and blame at the Yale Union, where I encountered a politically diverse good-natured, and superbly intelligent collection of intellectual provocateurs. My daughter Rachel Nussbaum Wichert discusses the national situation with me with her characteristic wit and incisiveness, and her husband Gerd Wichert adds the perspective of an immigrant, who embraces the US with love, problems and all.

The road toward writing this book began with Scott

Stephens's religion/culture blog in Australia, which posted my nascent thoughts while I was still in Japan. My agent Sydelle Kramer helped me in countless ways throughout the publication process. And Jon Karp has been a superbly insightful and responsive editor.

About the Author

MARTHA C. NUSSBAUM is the Ernst Freund Distinguished Service Professor of Law and Ethics, appointed in the Philosophy Department and the Law School of the University of Chicago. She gave the 2017 Jefferson Lecture for the National Endowment for the Humanities and has received both the 2016 Kyoto Prize in Arts and Philosophy, regarded as the most prestigious award available in fields not eligible for a Nobel, and the 2018 Don M. Randel Award for Achievement in the Humanities. She has written more than twenty-two books, including *Upheavals of Thought: The Intelligence of Emotions*; *Anger and Forgiveness: Resentment, Generosity, Justice*; *Not for Profit: Why Democracy Needs the Humanities*; and many more.